S0-BVP-387

WORLD
METAL
MARKETS

WORLD METAL MARKETS

The United States
Strategic Stockpile and
Global Market Influence

PATRICIA E. PERKINS

PRAEGER

Westport, Connecticut
London

Library of Congress Cataloging-in-Publication Data

Perkins, Patricia E.
World metal markets : the United States strategic stockpile and
global market influence / by Patricia E. Perkins.
p. cm.
Includes bibliographical references and index.
ISBN 0–275–94258–9 (alk. paper)
1. Metal trade. 2. Metal trade—United States. 3. Strategic
materials. 4. Strategic materials—United States. 5. Market
surveys. 6. Market surveys—United States. I. Title.
HD9506.A2P44   1997
382'.42'0973—dc21   96–47617

British Library Cataloguing in Publication Data is available.

Library of Congress Catalog Card Number: 96–47617
ISBN: 0–275–94258–9

First published in 1997

Praeger Publishers, 88 Post Road West, Westport, CT 06881
An imprint of Greenwood Publishing Group, Inc.

Printed in the United States of America

The paper used in this book complies with the
Permanent Paper Standard issued by the National
Information Standards Organization (Z39.48–1984).

10 9 8 7 6 5 4 3 2 1

Contents

Tables and Figures

Preface

Metals account for a relatively small proportion of global trade—less than 5 percent by value of total world exports, as compared with about 9 percent for food and about 65 percent for machinery and manufactured goods.[1] However, metals' actual importance in the global economy is disguised by these figures.

In the first place, the geographic distribution of mineral deposits makes self-sufficiency in metals less possible than in agricultural or manufactured goods, for nearly all countries.[2] Some countries depend heavily on metal exports to sustain their position in the world trading system; others are perpetual importers.

While substitution between metals, and shifts from primary sources to secondary (recycled) supplies of the same metal, helps consumers deal with periodic shortages,[3] there are no known substitutes for some metals in some uses—such as lead for nuclear shielding. Technological change has reduced the demand for some metals over the last few decades (tin in food packaging, for example), but increased the demand for others (cobalt for batteries, and vanadium for superconducting ceramics). In general, technological advances tend to increase the variety of minerals and metals required in the economy.[4]

Moreover, metals are crucial components of the machinery and infrastructure used to produce many other traded and nontraded goods, including food and other agricultural and resource-based products. The economic importance of metals extends far beyond their value as primary goods.

World metals consumption has grown exponentially in the 1900s.[5] Metals use began to fall off in comparison with GNP growth, however, beginning around 1970, as markets for consumer durables and many kinds of machinery became saturated in the North, and metal packaging materials were substituted by plastics and paper.[6] While overall world demand for metals is expected to grow as demand increases in the South, analysts are divided regarding the long-term global picture.

For example, are nonrenewable resources like oil, which is a raw material for plastics, only temporary substitutes for metals? And/or is oil a complement of metals, which are heavily energy-intensive in mining and smelting processes? In either case, metals production in a post-fossil fuel age will have to be drastically different from today.[7]

Although commercially exploitable mineral deposits represent only about 1 percent of the earth's crust,[8] minerals are quite widely distributed over the earth. New mining technologies and changing demand for different metals, among other factors, are continually changing the proportion of deposits which are considered "economic" compared to those which are "sub-economic."[9] Absolute shortages of mineral ores, while they are a long-term possibility, probably do not represent the principal factor limiting human metals use. Instead, political and/or environmental factors are likely to assume ever-increasing importance.

Metals provide one of the clearest examples of the process by which environmental ravages become economic gains: by digging up ores and adding energy, "free" rocks are converted into salable commodities. Governments everywhere subsidize this process. The environmental and social costs of mining, smelting, and recycling—using metals and distributing wastes containing them across the planet—seldom enter into prices because these environmental and social costs are usually externalized.[10] Pollution and limited terrestrial waste assimilation capacity will certainly limit metals use and raise prices in coming decades.[11]

Environmental limits may also combine with political limits on metals use in the decades to come. As this study helps to document, trade is an extremely political means of evening out geographical disparities in minerals supplies.[12] Minerals exploration, mining, and production are affected more by politics than by economic or geophysical efficiency.[13] Political scientist David G. Haglund notes, "Access to minerals continues to be ultimately a function of political processes, and because of this the access question remains today what it was in the 1930s, a matter of 'geopolitical' concern."[14]

From the earliest days of imperialism and global exploration by Europeans, metals have been a major goal and impetus; they have also helped to provide the technological means by which certain humans asserted their power over others.[15] Pricing in world markets is key to the social and political system by which transfers of metals around the world are implemented and rationalized. Metal transactions, however, have never been competitive or "free." Nearly all metal markets are highly oligopolistic; vast, diversified corporations exert market control through transfer pricing and verticalization of entire metal industries.[16] While the profits of metals multinationals are huge, they pale in comparison with the overall benefits of access to world metals resources for a relative few consumers in the North (and Southern elites).

World markets for industrial metals simultaneously provide the *evidence* of how these political processes are worked out, and also the *vehicle* by which they are mediated. The price on the world market, and what affects it, gives a glimpse of both economic and "geopolitical" activity.

It is in this global "geopolitical,"[17] environmental, and social context that I have undertaken to study the economic and, to some extent, political implications of metals stockpiling by the world's largest stockpiler, the United States. My goal is not particularly to demonstrate the huge market influence of metal consumers and producers in the United States, or to show that this influence is exerted via government channels as well as corporate ones and that the idea of "free markets" for industrial metals is patently ridiculous (which is clear in any case to all who investigate the subject). My main interest is in the details of interactions between public and private sector actors in the market, the way political considerations are brought to bear in specific situations, and the complexities of bargaining processes for control of metals.

In researching this book, I have come across many stories which I find fascinating; I hope that they will also be of interest to others. The more traditional statistical analysis included in the appendix aims to help demonstrate the overall significance of the sorts of market influences which are discussed in the text.

NOTES

1. U.N. Department for Economic and Social Information and Policy Analysis, Statistics Division, *1994 International Trade Statistics Yearbook,* Vol. II, Trade by Commodity (New York: United Nations, 1995), S102.

2. See David Haglund, "The New Geopolitics of Minerals: An Inquiry into the Changing International Significance of Strategic Minerals," *Political Geography Quarterly* 5, no. 3 (July 1986): 222.

3. Edward R. Fried, "International Trade in Raw Materials: Myths and Realities," *Science* 191 (1976): 643.

4. Haglund, 232.

5. Donald G. Rogich, "Changing Minerals and Material Use Patterns," speech presented to the Recycling Council of Ontario's 15th Annual Conference, October 5–7, 1994; Clive Ponting, *A Green History of the World* (New York: Penguin, 1991), 326–28.

6. John E. Tilton, *World Metal Demand: Trends and Prospects* (Washington, DC: Resources for the Future, 1991); Donald G. Rogich, "Changing Mineral and Material Use Patterns;" "Resource Firms Face Grim Reality," *Financial Post* (July 10, 1993); Carmine Nappi, *Metals Demand and the Canadian Metal Industry: Structural Changes and Policy Implications* (Kingston, Ontario: Queen's University, Centre for Resource Studies, 1989).

7. Metals were smelted in ancient times, beginning in what is now Swaziland about 43,000 years ago. (Judith Rees, *Natural Resources: Allocation, Economics and Policy,* London, New York: Routledge, 1990, 64). Wind-driven bellows were apparently used in ancient times in the Middle East to increase the efficiency of wood fires for smelting. The possibility and costs of high-volume metal smelting using solar power have yet to be demonstrated.

8. T. S. Lovering, *Minerals in World Affairs* (New York: Prentice-Hall, 1943), 127.

9. For an excellent discussion of the concepts of "reserves" and "resources," see Rees, 17–27. Bennett et al., in "A Systematic Approach to the Appraisal of National Mineral Supply" (in R. V. Ramani, *Application of Computer Methods in the Mineral Industry,* 1977), explain the resource categorization methodology used by the U.S. Bureau of Mines since 1975, called the Minerals Availability System.

10. See Rees, 49–55. The Mineral Policy Center in Washington, DC, which publishes a periodical called *Clementine*, has assembled extensive evidence concerning the environmental costs of mining in the United States; elsewhere the evidence of environmental problems connected with mining and use of metals similarly continues to mount.

11. For example, the Organization for Economic Cooperation and Development (OECD) in 1995 began discussions on guidelines for member countries in phasing out the hazardous metals lead, cadmium, and mercury for certain uses. See OECD, "Resolution of the Council Concerning the Declaration on Risk Reduction for Lead," Paris, March 21, 1996. See also "Mining Woes Blamed on Politics," *Toronto Star* (March 30, 1993); Paulo De Sa, "The European Non-Ferrous Metals Industry: 1993 and Beyond," *Resources Policy* 17, no. 3 (September 1991): 211–25.

12. Haglund, 234–36.

13. Rees, 60–75.

14. Haglund, 236–37. The "resource war" idea of the 1970s and 1980s, according to which the East Bloc was ostensibly maneuvering to cut the West off from supplies of strategic minerals (which tend to be geographically concentrated in Russia and Southern Africa), is one manifestation of the "geopolitics" of minerals trade issues. For discussion of the "resource war concept," see Haglund, *The New Geopolitics of Minerals: Canada and International Resource Trade* (Vancouver: University of British Columbia Press, 1989), 240–43; Al Gedicks, *The New Resource Wars* (Montreal: Black Rose Books, 1994), 41; Oye Ogunbadejo, *The International Politics of Africa's Strategic Minerals* (Westport, CT: Greenwood Press, 1985),181–97. Stated Haglund, writing in 1989, "It is conceivable, maybe likely, that Soviet foreign policy interests of a non-mineral nature will have an impact on mineral developments in southern Africa and elsewhere, but this hardly constitutes a basis for assuming that the USSR has launched a resource war: to infer from Soviet activity in Africa the existence of a resource-denial strategy is to commit the fallacy of mistaking correlation and consequence for motivation and cause" (244).

15. See Ponting, especially 216–23; also Ogunbadejo.

16. See Raymond F. Mikesell, *Nonfuel Minerals: Foreign Dependence and National Security* (Ann Arbor, MI: University of Michigan Press, 1987), 42–45.

17. Following Haglund's definition and explanation of this term.

Acknowledgments

In working on this project, I have benefitted from assistance and support of many different kinds. Professors Gerald K. Helleiner and David K. Foot provided much advice in the initial stages. Professor F. Gerard Adams and two anonymous reviewers commented on a partial, early draft. Jaime Tenho, Kwame Barko, and Pamela Leach also provided very useful comments. Workshop and conference participants at the University of Toronto and McMaster University, and colleagues at Ryerson Polytechnical University, York University, and the Universidade Eduardo Mondlane shared with me their feedback and insights. Todd Gordon, Cameron MacKay, Anders Hayden, Gord McDorman, Karl Hughes, Vincent Hildebrand, Chanda Meek, and David Boyd assisted with research and statistical work. Carina Hernandez, Pat McBain, and Marek Swinder helped to type and format the manuscript. A small research grant from the Social Sciences and Humanities Research Council of Canada paid some research costs, as did the Faculty of Environmental Studies at York University. Praeger editor Jim Ice was patient and supportive. I would also like to thank my parents, Henry and Ellen Perkins, my partner, Jess Poland, and my sons, Ben and Ned Poland, for their contributions of all kinds to the endeavor that has resulted in this book.

Abbreviations

ANMB	Army-Navy Munitions Board
AZI	American Zinc Institute (private)
BDSA	Business and Defense Services Administration
BFS	Bureau of Federal Supply
BOM	Bureau of Mines
CCC	Commodity Credit Corporation
CPA	Civilian Production Administration
CTC	Combined Tin Committee
DOD	Department of Defense
DPA	Defense Production Act
DRO	Defense Rated Order
ECA	Economic Cooperation Administration
ERP	European Recovery Program
FAA	Foreign Assistance Act
FBS	Federal Bureau of Supply
FEMA	Federal Emergency Management Agency
FPA	Federal Preparedness Agency
FPRS	Federal Property Resources Service (General Services Administration)
FSS	Federal Supply Service
GSA	General Services Administration
ITSG	International Tin Study Group (private)
LIA	Lead Industries Association (private)

MB	Munitions Board
MRC	Metals Reserve Company
NBS	National Bureau of Standards
NSRB	National Security Resources Board
ODC	Office of Domestic Commerce
OES	Office of Economic Stabilization
OIC	Office of Industry Cooperation
OMD	Office of Materials Distribution (U.S. Department of Commerce)
OMR	Office of Metals Reserve
OPA	Office of Price Administration
OTS	Office of Technical Services (U.S. Department of Commerce)
OWMR	Office of War Mobilization and Reconversion
RFC	Reconstruction Finance Corporation
USCC	United States Commercial Company
WAA	War Assets Administration
WAC	War Assets Corporation

All are (or were) agencies or programs of the United States government, unless indicated otherwise.

1

Introduction:
Industrial Metals in the World Economy,
the Strategic Stockpile,
and Market Dominance

At the beginning of the Cold War, the United States sought to secure adequate supplies of certain important industrial metals by establishing a "strategic stockpile." From the 1950s to the present, the U.S. stockpile has played a major role worldwide in metals exploration, development, and pricing. Along with U.S. government expenditures on military research and procurement, the space program, energy development, agriculture research, water diversions, and forest and rangeland management, the stockpile has been an important mechanism for government intervention in planning and shaping U.S.—and global—resource use and industrial development.

Now that the Cold War is over, the stockpile (along with many other pillars of U.S. policy) is coming under renewed scrutiny. Has it outlived its usefulness? What is its legacy, on balance? Is large-scale U.S. government involvement in metal markets desirable? What are the implications of abolishing the strategic stockpile? What are the considerations that must now enter into stockpile policy?

This study attempts to contribute to such a reassessment, first by examining the history of the U.S. strategic stockpile and its market effects in some detail, and second by discussing directions in stockpile policy as they relate to developments in the global markets for important industrial metals.

While plastics and ceramics are increasingly being used as substitutes for metals in some capacities, there is no question that industrial societies are still highly dependent on both basic metals and specialized alloys—just as they were at the time of World War II, when the stockpile was created to ensure self-sufficiency for the U.S. economy in case of a cutoff from external supplies of specified strategic metals.[1] Because the U.S. does not have supplies of all these metals within its boundaries, and since boycotts or war-related interruption of trade routes were predictable in wartime, there was widespread public support in the late 1940s and early 1950s for substantial investment in metals stocks by the U.S.

government. Whether such stocks serve any useful purpose in the 1990s is one of the issues under debate.

The U.S. stockpile now probably represents the largest body of salable commodities under the control of one market actor in the world. The stockpile has seldom played a role in meeting the defense needs of the United States, but sales of "surplus" commodities have often apparently served to dampen international price increases and, in a few cases, exacerbate price declines, while purchases for the stockpile have seemingly contributed to price increases for some metals.

Since it is both a purchaser and a supplier of stockpiled commodities on a large scale, and also the final consumer of many goods these commodities are used to produce, the U.S. government has arguably been for decades the single most important actor in many international metals markets. Its actions—not necessarily profit-maximizing or "rational" in an economic sense, and often determined primarily by domestic political considerations—are critically important in how these international metals markets work.

Such an understanding is important both for producer nations in their attempts to plan the efficient use of their resources and the overall growth path of their economies, and for consumer nations concerned with the availability and cost of resource supplies. Table 1.1 shows selected countries' export dependence on metal and mineral products. As "sustainability" moves to the forefront of policy discussions, the U.S. stockpile's market effects also merit consideration because of their possible ramifications for policies related to recycling, metals conservation, technological change, waste generation, and energy use—in the United States as well as other countries.

Discussions of the post-World War II history of international trade, for many different metals and other commodities that are held by the U.S. government,

Table 1.1
Metals and Minerals as a Percentage of Total Exports, Selected Countries, 1994

Country	Metals and Minerals	Percentage of Total Exports
Australia	lead, zinc, aluminum, bauxite	23.5
Bolivia	tin	16.7
Brazil	aluminum, bauxite, manganese	36.8
Canada	nickel, lead, aluminum, copper, molybdenum, cobalt	51.1
Chile	copper, molybdenum	34.2
Malaysia	tin	59.2
Peru	copper	28.0
Thailand	tin	39.0
Zimbabwe	chromium	25.6

Source: United Nations, *International Trade Statistics Yearbook* (New York: United Nations, 1995).

often mention the stockpile as one of the two or three most important factors influencing their markets. Yet the stockpile's administrators have repeatedly claimed they have lived up to their legislated mandate not to allow stockpile transactions to disrupt world markets.

The question of the stockpile's market effects is thus controversial, and it is further complicated by legal stipulations that "strategic" considerations be the only ones that enter into the stockpile decision-making process—despite the obvious potential for use of the government's enormous stocks of metals for "economic" purposes, e.g., price manipulation or stabilization.[2]

Another complication relates to the double opportunity for market influence which is created by the mechanics of the stockpile's operation: objectives for the amount of each metal the stockpile should hold are set in one governmental process, while actual sales and purchases to bring the stockpiled quantities into line with these goals are made at a later time, and with varying degrees of success or accuracy, by another set of actors within the U.S. government. Changes in both stockpile objectives and stockpile inventories can influence world markets.[3]

Although it was not until 1972 that a U.S. president openly cited "economic" reasons, not just "strategic" ones, in calling for a revision of stockpile goals,[4] the strategic stockpile clearly has long served more than just the defense purposes of the United States. Examples of stockpile transactions which have clearly involved nonmilitary considerations, and which have had important influences on world commodity markets, date back to the 1940s for a wide variety of metals. The many uncertainties of the legislative and bureaucratic process by which stockpile goals and inventories are determined also appear to have heightened the instability of international markets.

THE U.S. STRATEGIC STOCKPILE AND METAL MARKETS—KEY HISTORICAL ISSUES

The U.S. government made large-scale metals purchases through the mid-1950s to establish the strategic stockpile (see Table 1.2). These stockpile purchases generally kept world production levels for many metals much higher in the post–World War II years than they would otherwise have been, because of their price effects as well as their relationships with other U.S. government programs designed to stimulate and subsidize metals production.

The large U.S. government purchases temporarily staved off post–World War II decline in many basic metals industries. They also contributed to significant global overproduction of tin, copper, and other metals, causing economic and political problems once the U.S. purchases ceased.[5]

The stockpile inventories built up in the 1950s were huge; for some metals, they surpassed annual world production volumes (see Table 1.3, a comparison of the historical maximum stockpile inventory and world production in the same year for important industrial metals).

Table 1.2
Total Expenditures of Stockpiling Funds by Fiscal Year, 1947–1992

Year	Expenditures (U.S. Dollars)	Year	Expenditures (U.S. Dollars)
1947 and earlier	66,330,731	1970	13,799,261
1948	82,907,575	1971	15,797,095
1949	304,486,177	1972	17,077,779
1950	440,834,970	1973	15,710,849
1951	655,537,199	1974	19,359,315
1952	844,683,459	1975	13,923,141
1953	906,158,850	1976	9,115,170
1954	644,760,321	1977	8,484,007
1955	801,310,094	1978	8,803,194
1956	382,011,786	1979*	0
1957	354,576,558	1980	0
1958	173,753,997	1981	78,038,392
1959	65,260,098	1982†	41,900,000
1960	49,227,142	1983	145,200,000
1961	33,325,431	1984	108,800,000
1962	33,695,431	1985	8,700,000
1963	22,104,176	1986	18,902,000
1964	16,091,067	1987	1,100,000
1965	16,561,275	1988	115,095,555
1966	16,468,100	1989	139,150,000
1967	17,981,675	1990	55,143,670
1968	15,902,213	1991	219,096,261
1969	15,914,729	1992	294,863,439

Source: U.S. General Services Administration, Office of Preparedness, *Stockpile Report to the Congress,* various years; U.S. Department of Defense, *Report to the Congress on National Defense Stockpile Requirements,* various years.

* Beginning in 1979, only expenditures on commodity purchases for the stockpile are included. Prior to 1979, figures also reflect stockpile management and maintenance costs, which were not reported after 1979.

† For 1982 and subsequent years, these figures are estimates based on information reported on a commodity-by-commodity basis.

Table 1.3

Comparison of Historical Maximum Stockpile Inventory and World Production of Eleven Metals

Metal	Year	Stockpile Inventory	World Production	Percentage*
Aluminum (million short tons)	1963	1,981	6,095	33
Bauxite (million long tons)	1965	16,749	36,849	46
Chromite (million short tons)	1964	6,339	4,583	138
Copper (million short tons)	1960	1,151	4,650	25
Cobalt (million pounds)	1960	10,326	31,400	33
Lead (million short tons)	1961	1,386	2,665	52
Manganese (million short tons)	1965	10,780	19,557	55
Molybdenum (million pounds)	1956	84,607	70,400	120
Nickel (million short tons)	1959	242	314	77
Tin (million long tons)	1960	352	180.4	195
Zinc (million short tons)	1962	1,581	3,750	38

Source: U.S. Bureau of Mines, *Minerals Yearbook*, various issues.

* Stockpile inventory expressed as a percentage of world production.

In general, the United States began in the 1960s to reduce the desired size of the strategic stockpile and sell off these metals stocks, although there were also several subsequent upward revisions of stockpile goals and purchases of particular metals. Figures 1.1 through 1.11 provide a graphical representation of U.S. stockpile objectives, inventories, and world prices for the same metals over the period 1947–1991. Noteworthy are the wide divergencies between stockpile objectives and actual inventories for all metals throughout the period; in fact there are almost no instances in which the stockpile actually held its professed objective amount of any commodity. Also apparent in these figures are the periods where sales by the stockpile (a downward-trending "inventory" line) coincide with falling metal prices, or where purchases coincide with price increases. These can be viewed as periods where stockpile transactions heightened price trends and helped to destabilize the market.

Metals sales by the U.S. government had an anti-inflationary impact, especially during the Vietnam War years. In specific instances, stockpile policy was explicitly used to forestall or prevent producer price increases (e.g., for aluminum and copper

Figure 1.1
Aluminum Objective, Inventory and Price

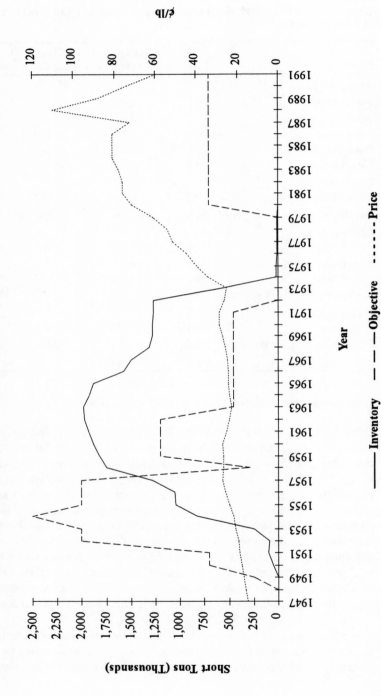

Figure 1.2
Bauxite Objective, Inventory and Price

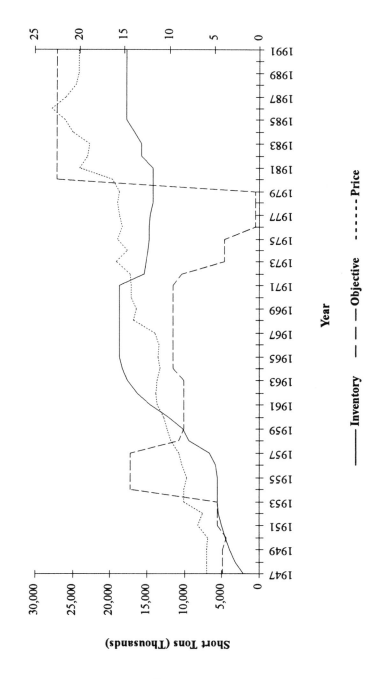

Figure 1.3
Chromite Objective, Inventory and Price

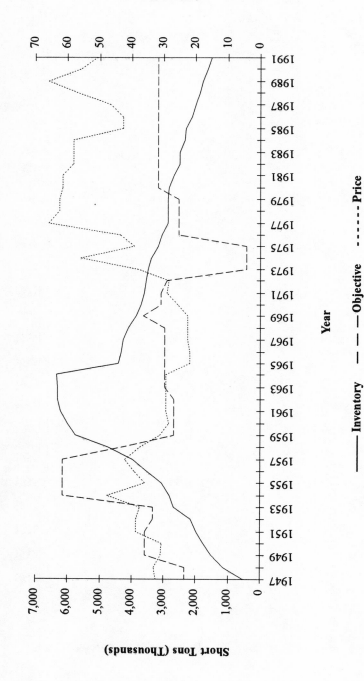

Figure 1.4
Cobalt Objective, Inventory and Price

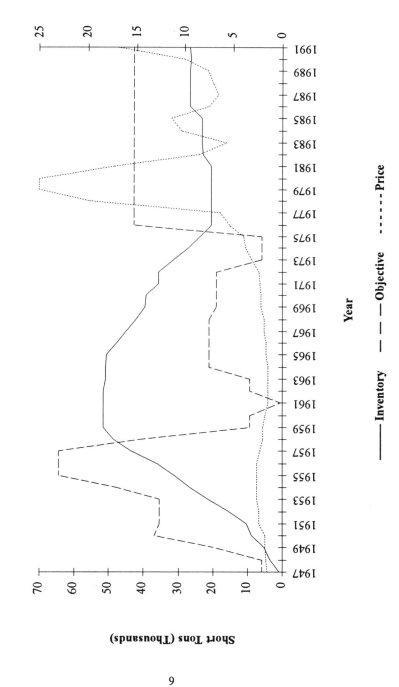

Figure 1.5
Copper Objective, Inventory and Price

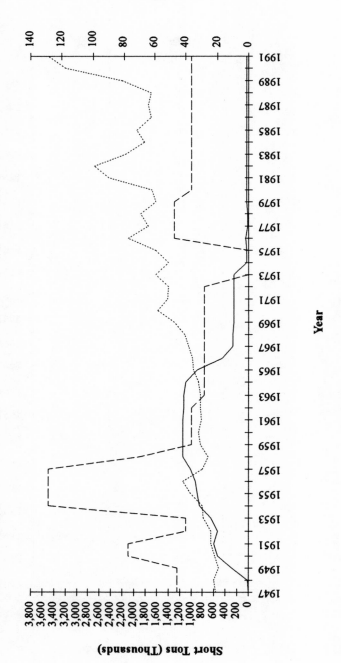

Year

—— Inventory   — — Objective   ······ Price

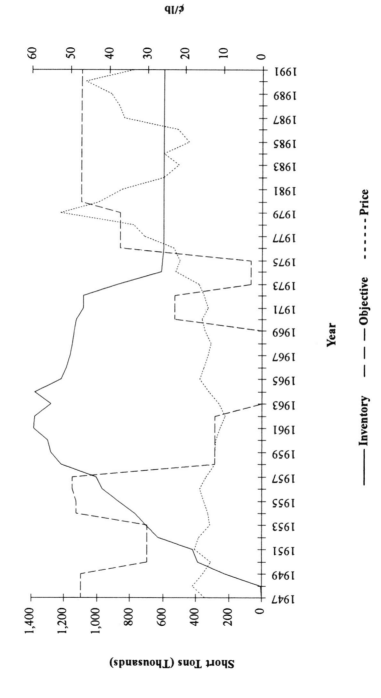

Figure 1.6
Lead Objective, Inventory and Price

——— Inventory   — — —Objective   · · · · · · Price

Year

¢/lb

Short Tons (Thousands)

11

Figure 1.7
Manganese Objective, Inventory and Price

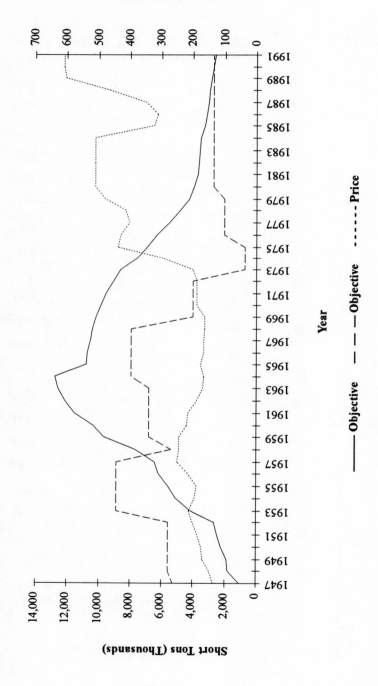

Figure 1.8
Molybdenum Objective, Inventory and Price

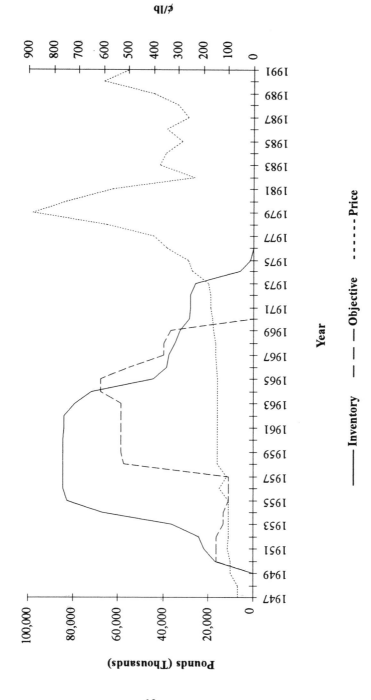

Figure 1.9
Nickel Objective, Inventory and Price

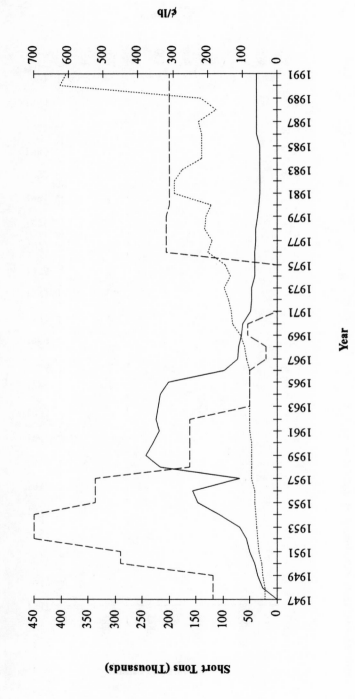

Year

——— Inventory   — — —Objective   · · · · · ·Price

14

Figure 1.10
Tin Objective, Inventory and Price

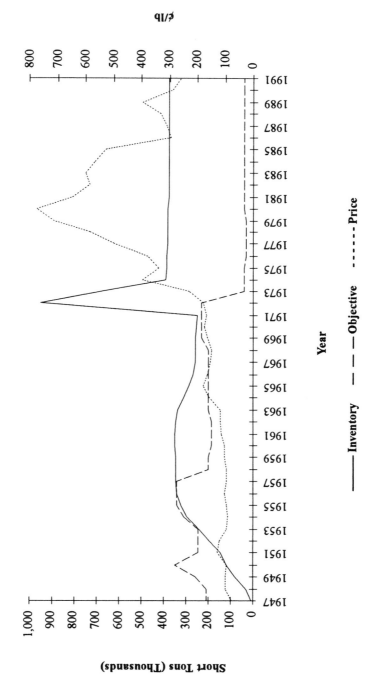

Figure 1.11
Zinc Objective, Inventory and Price

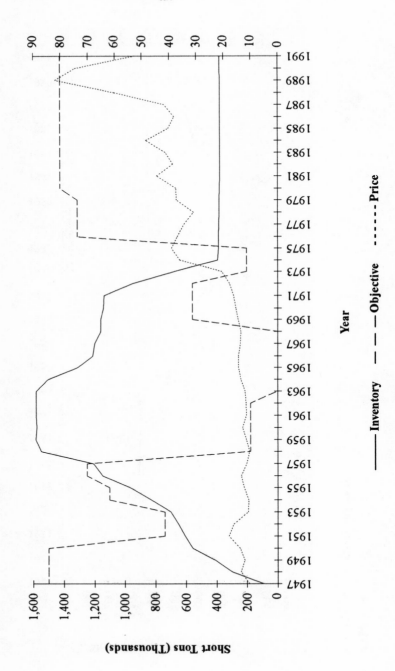

¢/lb

Short Tons (Thousands)

Year

——— Inventory   — — — Objective   · · · · · · Price

in 1965, lead and zinc in 1970, and tin in 1980–1981). In other cases, stockpile purchases were part of broader government programs to assist metals producers and stimulate domestic production (e.g., for chromium, manganese, and cobalt in the early 1950s and copper in 1978), or to assist producer nations abroad for foreign policy reasons (e.g., chromium acquired from Turkey in 1955, cobalt from Rhodesia in 1961–1962, and bauxite from Jamaica in the early 1980s).

Thus, the general pattern of the stockpile's market impact was one of demand-side stimulation through the mid-1950s, followed by supply-side contributions (or "threats" to sell) in the subsequent period. However, the stockpile has influenced metal markets in a wide variety of ways over the fifty years of its existence. The purpose of this book, as noted above, is to review and analyze these market effects, both for individual markets and in the aggregate, and to discuss the stockpile's role and market influence in the context of the late 1990s.

OVERVIEW OF THE BOOK

Chapter 2 provides an introduction to the U.S. government agencies and institutions that are involved in making and carrying out stockpile policy, as well as the major shifts in stockpile policy and legislation that have taken place over the years. An overview of the stockpile's history follows, in chapters 3 and 4. Aspects of stockpile policy that go beyond military-related considerations are discussed in the next two chapters: domestic political factors, foreign policy, and metal market disruption. Case studies of stockpile policy and market effects in relation to several specific metals are then examined, in chapters 7 through 11. The final chapter summarizes the study's main points and offers a few concluding remarks.

NOTES

1. For a thorough discussion of what "strategic minerals" are, and how the usage of this term has changed over time, see David G. Haglund, *The New Geopolitics of Minerals: Canada and International Resource Trade* (Vancouver: University of British Columbia Press, 1989), 222–37.

2. See Judith Rees, *Natural Resources: Allocation, Economics and Policy* (London, New York: Routledge, 1990), 171.

3. Throughout this book, "inventory" means the actual amount of the metal which the U.S. federal government has on hand at a given point in time as part of its stockpile; "objective" or "goal" means the desired amount which the government has stated the strategic stockpile *should* contain at that point in time, as set by executive-branch agencies with input from Congress and the presidential administration.

4. U.S. Congress, Joint Committee on Banking. *Hearings: Defense Industrial Base, Part 3: New Stockpile Objectives.* 94th Congress, 2nd session, November 24, 1976.

5. See, for example, William Fox, *Tin: The Working of a Commodity Agreement* (London: Mining Journal Books, 1974), 242. Some tin-producing interests, at least, did express unease at the implications of the United States' formation of such huge stocks, because of the bargaining power they gave the U.S. vis-à-vis the International Tin Council; provisions on the eventual liquidation of the stock pile were inserted in the International

Tin Agreement. They limited the amount of tin the United States could release any one year to 5,000 tons or 5 percent of the aggregate tin stockpile, whichever was less, and they required the United States to give ITC at least three months' notice of any planned sales. (See K. E. Knorr, *Tin Under Control,* Stanford, CA: Food Research Institute, 1945, 180.) The United States did not join ITC, and thus did not formally submit to such constrains on its tin stockpile disposal, until 1976—and then only briefly.

Part I

Stockpile History and Policy

Historical context is necessary in order to situate the subsequent discussion of the strategic stockpile's market effects.* The following three chapters provide a historical overview of the legal foundations of the stockpile, its growth following World War II, and how it has been managed over time.

* For histories of the U.S. strategic stockpile, see Frederick J. Dobney, "Stockpiling and Shortages," *Social Science Quarterly* 57 (Spring 1976): 455–65; Raymond F. Mikesell, *Stockpiling Strategic Materials: An Evaluation of the National Program* (1986); and James A. McClure, "Stockpiling of Strategic and Critical Materials," *Idaho Law Review* 19 (1983): 417–53.

2

The Stockpile's Institutional and Legal Framework

The idea of stockpiling by the U.S. government as a means of preventing war-related market interruptions for important military commodities dates back at least to World War I. However, it was not until the late 1930s that appropriations were made by Congress for this purpose. Special emphasis was placed on four materials—manganese ore, chrome ore, tungsten ore, and tin—because of U.S. dependence on imports of these metals.[1] The events of World War II essentially overtook the stockpiling program, and by the end of the war, the list of commodities which the U.S. Munitions Board felt were needed in the stockpile had grown to include 67 materials in the most important category and an additional 39 in a secondary category.[2] Today the stockpile contains 107 different commodities (see Table 2.1).[3]

Table 2.1
List of Commodities Currently Stockpiled by the United States

Aluminum Group
  Aluminum Metal
  Bauxite, Metal Grade, Group
  Bauxite, Metal Grade, Jamaica Type
  Bauxite, Metal Grade, Surinam Type
Aluminum Oxide
  Aluminum Oxide, Abrasive Grain
  Aluminum Oxide, Fused, Crude
Antimony
Asbestos
  Amosite
  Chrysotile
Bauxite, Refractory

Beryllium Metal
  Beryl Ore
  Beryllium Copper Master Alloy
  Beryllium Metal
Bismuth
Cadmium
Chromite, Refractory Grade
Chromium Group
  Chromite, Chemical and Metal Group
  Chromite, Chemical Grade
  Chromite, Metallurgical Grade
  Chromium, Ferro Group
  Chromium, Ferro, High Carbon
  Chromium, Ferro, Low Carbon

Table 2.1: (continued)

Chromium, Ferro, Silicon
Chromium Metal
Cobalt
Columbium Group
  Columbium Carbide Powder
  Columbium Concentrates
  Columbium, Ferro
  Columbium, Metal
Diamond, Industrial
  Diamond Dies
  Diamond, Industrial, Crushing Boart
  Diamond, Industrial, stones
Fluorspar
  Acid Grade
  Metallurgical Grade
Germanium
Graphite
  Ceylon Amorphous (Lump)
  Malagasy (Crystalline)
  Other than Ceylon & Malagasy
Indium
Iodine
Jewel Bearings
  Jewel Bearings
  Jewel Bearings—NSG
  Sapphire and Ruby
Lead
Manganese Dioxide Battery Grade
  Manganese Dioxide, Battery Grade,
  Natural
  Manganese Dioxide, Battery Grade,
  Synthetic
Manganese Group
  Manganese Ore Group
  Manganese Ore, Chemical Grade
  Manganese Ore, Metallurgical Grade
  Manganese, Ferro Group
  Manganese, Ferro, High Carbon
  Manganese, Ferro, Medium Carbon
  Manganese, Ferro, Silicon
  Manganese Metal (Electrolytic)
Mercury

Mica
  Muscovite Block, Stained and Better
  Muscovite Film, 1st and 2nd Qualities
  Muscovite Splittings
  Phlogopite Block
  Phlogopite Splittings
Morphine Sulfate (Refined)
Nickel
Platinum Group Metals
  Iridium
  Palladium
  Platinum
Quartz Crystals
Quinidine
Quinine
Ricinoleic/Sebacic Acid Products
Rubber, Natural
Rutile
Silicon Carbide
Silver
Talc, Steatite Block & Lump
Tantalum Group
  Tantalum Carbide Powder
  Tantalum Metal Powder
  Tantalum Metal
  Tantalum Minerals
  Tantalum Oxide
Thorium Nitrate
Tin
Titanium Sponge
Tungsten Group
  Tungsten Carbide Powder
  Tungsten, Ferro
  Tungsten Metal Powder
  Tungsten Ores & Concentrates
Vanadium Pentoxide
Vegetable Tannin Extract
  Chestnut
  Quebracho
  Wattle
Zinc

Source: U.S. Department of Defense, *Strategic and Critical Materials Report to the Congress: Operations under the Strategic and Critical Materials Stock Piling Act during the Period October 1994 through September 1995* (Washington, DC: January 1996), 24–26.

EARLY STOCKPILE LEGISLATION

Legislation establishing the U.S. strategic stockpile, called the Strategic and Critical Materials Stock Piling Act, was passed in 1939, amended in 1946, and then thoroughly revised in 1979. Further amendments followed in 1981. The full text of the 1946 Act appears in Appendix A, along with subsequent revisions.

Of special interest are the provisions of the Stock Piling Act requiring the stockpile's managers to give "due regard" to "the protection of producers, processors, and consumers against avoidable disruption of their usual markets" (Section 3(e)) and to release materials from the stockpile only "(a) on the order of the President at any time when in his judgment such release is required for purposes of the common defense, or (b) in time of war or during a national emergency with respect to common defense proclaimed by the President, on order of such agency as may be designated by the President" (Section 5). One of the focuses of this study concerns how well these provisions have been carried out—or indeed, how possible it is to carry out such provisions.

Despite the fact that the stockpile's main purpose was to store commodities that the U.S. did *not* produce, the 1939 and 1946 acts included "buy American" provisions which required the stockpile to purchase materials mined or produced in the United States, unless this was determined to be "inconsistent with the public interest, or the cost to be unreasonable."[4] Presumably included at the behest of Congress members from districts that did or could produce stockpiled commodities, this provision was dropped in the 1979 revisions to the Act.

In the 1946 Act, stockpile purchases were required to be "made, so far as is practicable, from supplies of materials in excess of the current industrial demand"; this was intended to prevent adverse effects on U.S. industries that were still producing at high levels in the postwar years.

Two pieces of U.S. legislation enacted in the early 1950s had the effect of forcing the stockpile to act quite differently from a profit-maximizing firm or an economic buffer stock, thus complicating its influences on metal markets. These were the Defense Production Act (DPA) of 1950 (which provided subsidies for U.S. mining and other industries, some of which were implemented via stockpile transactions) and the Agricultural Trade Development and Assistance Act of 1954 (which subsidized U.S. farmers by creating export markets for their products, also implemented in part via stockpile barter and other transactions). These programs are discussed in more detail in the following chapter.

1979 AND 1981 REVISIONS TO STOCKPILE LEGISLATION

The 1946 act establishing the stockpile was completely rewritten and revised by the passage of P.L. 96-41, the Strategic and Critical Materials Stock Piling Revision Act, in 1979. This legislation expanded the U.S. stockpiling program to include the commodities necessary to meet civilian needs—as well as military ones—of the United States in times of national emergency. Strong language was, however, inserted to reduce the potential market impact of the stockpiling program: "The purpose of the stockpile is to serve the interest of national defense only and is not be used for economic or budgetary purposes."[5]

For the first time, the minimum period for which stockpiled commodities were to be expected to meet U.S. demand was specified in the 1979 act: three years. The act also defined the terms "strategic and critical materials" and "national emergency."

Its largest change, however, related to the procedures outlined for administering stockpile transactions. In a sense, the 1979 act increased the importance of the President, Congress, *and* the General Services Administration (GSA) in stockpile policy. The President was granted authority to determine two key criteria for stockpile disposals: first, that the materials to be sold are in excess of stockpile requirements, and second, that failure to sell them would cause loss to the Treasury. Congress' specific authorization was required for all stockpile acquisitions; no blanket authorizations were to be allowed as previously. The GSA would control the day-to-day use of a separate fund established in the Treasury to handle all stockpile receipts and expenditures. This would prevent receipts from flowing into general Treasury revenues; purchases of stockpile commodities would have to be made with the proceeds from stockpile sales.

Two "sunset" rules were attached to the use of this Defense Stockpile Transactions Fund: "If sales proceeds rest there for three years without being appropriated by Congress at the stockpile managers' request, they will revert to general revenues and be lost. Similarly, if, after appropriation, the funds are not spent for stockpile acquisitions within five years, they will again have to revert to general revenues and will no longer be earmarked for stockpile acquisitions."[6]

The goal of these changes was apparently to balance the stockpile's potential for use to curry political favors against its potential for market influence. By mandating competitive, above-board transactions on the part of the GSA, and giving stockpile managers several years to ride out market fluctuations in order to "buy cheap," the legislation aimed to minimize the cost of stockpile acquisitions. At the same time, it provided for fairly tight Congressional controls and approvals of general stockpile policy, thus allowing for some political buffering of stockpile managers' actions.[7] The rhetoric surrounding the 1979 act's implementation was that it "opens a new era in stockpile management."[8]

Amendments to the 1979 act were included as part of the Omnibus Budget Reconciliation Act of 1981. The time limits stipulated for funds' availability within the National Defense Stockpile Transaction Fund were eliminated, effectively preventing receipts from stockpile sales from *ever* being used for non-stockpile related purposes. The 1981 amendments increased Congressional oversight of stockpile management in several other ways as well.[9]

LEGISLATIVE CHANGES IN THE 1980s

In 1985, the Reagan administration proposed a 95 percent reduction in the stockpile objective levels legislated in 1979, effectively reducing the stockpile to eleven minerals, with sixteen more in a "supplemental reserve."[10] While this policy appeared to some inconsistent with the administration's pro-military stance, it represented a "government out of stockpiling" position of the sort advocated for decades by much of the metals industry. It was based on a study by the National Security Council which recommended that stockpiles should only be relied upon for partial military mobilization, since U.S. allies would be able to supplement domestically held metals supplies. Budgetary considerations—the financial benefits of selling off stockpiled commodities—were also cited by administration officials.[11]

The stockpile reduction proposal met with heavy political resistance, and a decision was put off until 1988. In that year, rather than directly reducing stockpile objectives, Reagan transferred responsibility for managing the stockpile to the Department of Defense. By 1992, the Pentagon was stating that the three-year conventional war requirements set out in the Strategic and Critical Materials Stock Piling Act implied "planning estimates far larger than the national security needs required by our new post-cold war planning assumptions," and that the Defense Department would be submitting a legislative proposal to reduce the three-year war requirement and authorize the sale of up to $1 billion in "excess inventories."[12]

In 1993, although a three-year war planning scenario was still employed, the Pentagon's estimate of the amounts of materials needed in the stockpile continued to drop. This was because "a greatly enhanced mobilization period of three to five years" was put forward, "based on an updated threat assessment development after the dissolution of the Soviet Union."[13] The longer mobilization time, stated the Defense Department, would allow U.S. "capacity enhancement after a ramp-up period."[14]

STOCKPILE MANAGEMENT AND OBJECTIVE SETTING

When the stockpile was first established, it was run by the U.S. War and Navy Departments. From the early 1950s until 1988, the day-to-day management of the stockpile was the responsibility of the civil service staff of the Federal Preparedness Agency (FPA) or its successor agency, the Federal Emergency Management Agency (FEMA), within the (GSA), which is the U.S. agency responsible for managing most government-owned property. In early 1988, as noted above, responsibility for administering the stockpile was again transferred to the Department of Defense.

In general, until 1988, the stockpile management procedure was as follows. Based on information it solicited and received from U.S. private industry and from the State, Commerce, Interior, and Defense departments, the FPA/FEMA decided what commodities should be stockpiled and in what quantities, changing these objectives to conform to changing defense and other technologies. The objectives were set within the overall framework directives of stockpile policy, such as the length of time for which the stockpile was designed to supply U.S.

needs; these general directives were drawn up by the presidential administration, subject to Congressional approval. The GSA also handled the purchases and sales necessary to rotate stocks and keep the stockpile up-to-date.

The adjustment between objectives and inventories for each commodity was far from instantaneous, however, and there were no time constraints on the GSA's activities or sanctions if inventories were not brought into line with objectives within a given period. In fact, the periods when inventories and objectives were equal seem the exception rather than the rule for most metals (see Figures 1.1 through 1.11, chapter 1). Contributing to these lags were the delays inherent in the Congressional budgetary process. Barring a presidentially declared national emergency, sales could only be made from the "excess" materials available when stockpile inventories exceeded objectives, and then only with Congressional permission—which often, but not always, followed an initiative by the GSA or the President to make the sales. Purchases for the stockpile were usually made at the initiative of the GSA or the administration, though Congress could also suggest or mandate an acquisition (and in all cases had to appropriate funds for it).[15]

The President retained the power to issue overall directives on stockpile policy and to specify the length of time for which a cutoff from external commodity supply sources was envisioned. Periodically, broad new sets of directives were issued, sometimes at Congress' urging. Between 1947 and 1971, for example, such policy revisions resulted in ninety-four separate adjustments to the objectives for stockpiled forms of eleven important industrial metals (see Figure 2.1).

Throughout the period, U.S. government officials repeatedly insisted that the stockpile objectives, as intended by the legislation establishing the stockpile, were based purely on national defense considerations and on the amounts of the commodity required in order to keep the U.S. economy functioning in wartime.

A document prepared by the Federal Emergency Management Agency, dated November 15, 1976 and entitled "Methodology of Estimating Stockpile Goals," described the following procedure for setting stockpile objectives. U.S. industrial demand was divided into three "tiers"—defense, essential civilian and general civilian—and each tier was assigned a priority and a risk coefficient, reflecting the government's "willingness to accept risk of not meeting the wartime needs" of that tier. Industrial demand for a wartime period was estimated using projections of peacetime demand, interest rates, corporate retained earnings, and estimates of expected civilian austerity, reallocations of consumer demand toward nondurable goods and services and of investment toward war production, restructuring of imports and exports, and defense expenditure patterns. There was obviously a wide margin of choice in all these estimates; they were "developed by inter-agency working groups and reviewed by an Inter-Agency Steering Committee before being employed in the methodology."[16] Wartime GNP estimates were fed through an input-output table, to generate consumption estimates for each stockpiled commodity for the length of the national emergency envisioned. These were modified, based on the shortfall-risk-by-tier factors, and materials substitution possibilities were also considered.

Figure 2.1
Adjustments to Stockpile Objectives for Eleven Metals, 1947–1991

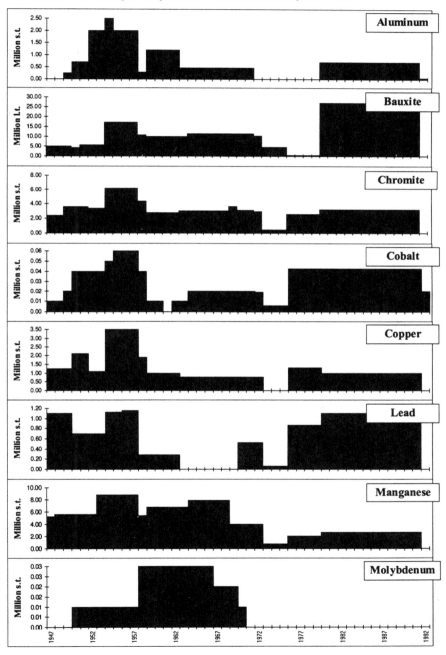

Figure 2.1: (continued)

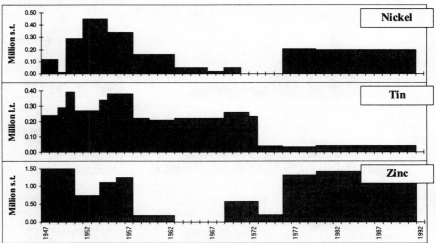

The supply of stockpiled materials available from producer nations was also estimated, based on normal supply patterns, expanded production possibilities, and "political reliability." The latter was estimated by rating producer nations on the following criteria: "political orientation toward the U.S., ability to sustain stockpile material exports in wartime, dependability of the labor force in wartime, (and) vulnerability to sabotage. The(se) ratings (were) done by State Department desk officers with higher level review."[17]

Estimates of shortfalls of requirements versus supplies generated the "unadjusted stockpile goals," which were then evaluated and modified in light of "special circumstances," such as high defense-related uses or high U.S. import dependence. The agencies involved in this final stockpile goal adjustment process are not named in the document.

In sum, an elaborate procedure was used for generating stockpile objectives, but its results were subject to discretionary modification by the administration in the final stages before the objectives were announced.

The 1976 FEMA document seems to represent a codification of the stockpile objective-setting procedure employed over much of the postwar period. A description of much the same process is found in Congressional testimony twenty years earlier by Arthur S. Flemming, director of the GSA's Office of Defense Mobilization:

We go through a rather formal procedure in establishing those objectives.

We do get military requirements from the Department of Defense; we get the defense or war-supporting requirements from the appropriate delegate agency, Commerce, Interior, as the case may be, as well as the requirements for a rockbottom submitted economy [sic].

And then we balance that over against supply.

What could we expect to get through normal channels after we had moved into a period of general mobilization?

In the case of the minimum stockpile, we estimate what we could get from domestic sources, and also what we could get from foreign sources.

The foreign sources of supply are discounted on the basis of strategic advice given to us by the Joint Chiefs of Staff and by the Department of State.

Then, having determined the requirements, determined what would be available in the way of supply, one is balanced over against the other.

We determine what the gap would be over a 5-year emergency period, and, having determined what that gap would be, that becomes our stockpile objective, minimum stockpile objective.

Now, in the case of the long-term stockpile objectives, we discount our foreign sources of supply 100 percent, except in the case of Canada, Mexico, and a few countries in the Caribbean area. Those objectives, of course, are open to scrutiny at any time on the part of any committee of the Congress. It has to be done in executive session because of the classified nature of the material, but that can always be done....

Now, in setting out the long-term stockpile policy the President did say that, having reached our minimum stockpile objective, we were to move toward our long-term stockpile objective, at times when we could acquire the material under favorable conditions and when we by acquiring it could help to strengthen our domestic mobilization base, because there is not any question in our mind but that a strong domestic mobilization base, as far as many of these materials are concerned, is one of the very best safeguards that we have.

We can be just as careful as possible in setting our stockpile objectives, but they do reflect a subjective judgement on the part of a good many people all the way up the line. I meant starting back with your military requirements and coming right up the line, and someone could make a mistake, and he could make a mistake on the low side.[18]

From 1954 to 1970, the objective-setting process included "concentration factoring," or contingency planning to ensure adequate supplies if key domestic or Canadian production facilities were "lost" (due to bombing or sabotage) in wartime. The output of any plant that supplied more than 20 percent of U.S. emergency supply (this was changed to 25 percent in 1963) was partially discounted in the "concentration factoring" process for the period of time it would take to rebuild the plant if it were destroyed. When "concentration factoring" was discontinued by the Office of Emergency Preparedness in 1970 as nuclear strategy replaced conventional war strategy, this had the effect of lowering many metals' stockpile objectives.[19]

Following the transfer of stockpile management responsibility to the Department of Defense in 1988, the procedure for arriving at stockpile objectives was updated, but the same sort of technique employed previously—involving estimates of military, civilian, and industrial requirements—continued to be used. Estimates of the political reliability of foreign suppliers were much more elaborate than in earlier years. High level policy officials in the Department of Defense made the final modifications to the estimates.[20]

The picture that emerges of how stockpile objectives were set throughout most of the post–World War II period thus includes complex rules to guide bureaucrats in arriving at numerical targets, as well as the possibility of political manipulation of these targets by higher executive-branch officials. To see how the objectives related to actual purchases (or sales) of stockpiled commodities, we must proceed to a more detailed examination of the history of these transactions.

NOTES

1. James A. McClure, "Stockpiling of Strategic and Critical Materials," *Idaho Law Review* 19 (1983): 417–18.

2. Ibid., 422–25.

3. U.S. Department of Defense, *1992 Report to the Congress on National Defense Stockpile Requirements*, 13-1 to 13-6.

4. Ibid., 419.

5. See James A. McClure, "Stockpiling of Strategic and Critical Materials," 430–32. The full text of the 1979 act appears in the Appendix A.

6. Robert A. Cornell, "United States Stockpile Policy," 11.

7. Ibid., 13.

8. Ibid., 9.

9. See James A. McClure, "Stockpiling of Strategic and Critical Materials," 432–34.

10. "Resource Wars: The Myth of American Mineral Vulnerability," 43; Milton R. Copulas, *Securing America's Energy and Mineral Needs*, 48–49.

11. Ibid.

12. U.S. Department of Defense, *1992 Report to the Congress on National Defense Stockpile Requirements*, ES-1.

13. U.S. Department of Defense, *1993 Report to the Congress on National Defense Stockpile Requirements*, 2.

14. Ibid., 3.

15. More detail on the rules concerning stockpile disposals is contained in McClure, 426–27.

16. Federal Emergency Management Agency, "Methodology of estimating stockpile goals," 1976, 3.

17. Ibid., 7.

18. U.S. Congress, Senate, Select Committee on Small Business, Subcommittee No. 2. *Hearings: Problems Resulting from the Exclusion of Small Business from Stockpile Purchases and from Participation in the Disposal of Surplus Products Program*. 84th Congress, 2nd session, July 11, 12, and 17, 1956, 34.

19. U.S. Congress, Senate, Committee on Armed Services, Subcommittee on National Stockpile and Naval Petroleum Reserves. *Hearing: Disposals from National and Supplemental Stockpiles*. 91st Congress, 2nd session, February 27, 1970, 3. This source contains Congressional testimony of the Director of the Office of Emergency Preparedness, who noted that "the Department of Defense did not concur in this change [away from 'concentration factoring'] because experience in World War II and two limited wars did not provide a basis for such discounts." See also U.S. Congress, Senate, Committee on Armed Services, Subcommittee on National Stockpile and Naval Petroleum Reserves. *Hearing: Disposals from National and Supplemental Stockpiles*. 92nd Congress, 1st session, April 7, 1971, 43.

20. See U.S. Department of Defense, *1992 Report to the Congress on National Defense Stockpile Requirements*, February 1992, 1–7.

3

The Growth of the Stockpile

The accumulation of supplies to meet the stockpile's first objectives took more than ten years, continuing well into the 1960s for some commodities. This process was marked by a number of controversies, during which the important tensions and political issues that have characterized stockpile policy soon became apparent.

ACQUISITIONS AT HOME OR ABROAD?

In the years immediately following World War II, surplus government-owned supplies of strategic materials that had been accumulated during the war were transferred into the stockpile. The question of how to make up shortfalls between the resulting stockpile and the desired objectives sparked a domestic political debate—one of several ongoing struggles within the U.S. government concerning stockpile policy. As summarized by former Idaho Senator James McClure:

The State Department was opposed to giving any preference to the purchase of domestic minerals on the theory that it would be contradictory to its free-trade policy, arguing that any abrupt decline in United States purchasing of raw materials at the end of the war, with consequent disruption of economies of producing countries, would be harmful to the transition from wartime to peacetime demand.

The Department of the Interior, on the other hand, pressed for development of a large stockpile with a strong emphasis on purchases from the domestic industry, tight controls on disposals, and a transfer of all government-owned war surplus materials to the stockpile.[1]

The 1946 stockpile act created "industry advisory committees" to advise the Secretaries of War, Navy, and Interior on stockpiling procedures. As noted, it also included a "Buy American" provision requiring that purchases be made domestically, insofar as possible,[2] but modified this somewhat by also requiring that purchases be of "supplies ... in excess of current industrial demand"—a caveat intended to relieve pressure on U.S. industries which were still producing at close to wartime levels to meet the high postwar industrial demand.[3]

At the outbreak of the Korean War, the stockpile objectives were only about two-fifths complete. To encourage and expand U.S. production of strategic materials, on September 8, 1950 Congress passed the Defense Production Act. This gave the President broad powers to

issue priorities, allocate materials, prevent hoarding, control prices, buy and sell materials for current use, and offer incentives to expand production.... Within a few years, ... domestic aluminum production doubled, domestic copper mine capacity increased twenty-five percent, domestic nickel mining was initiated, a titanium industry was created, tungsten mining quadrupled, and the world columbium-tantalum mining and processing industries greatly expanded, not to mention the augmentation of supplies of many other materials for production needs and stockpiles.[4]

The Defense Production Act did not affect stockpiling *per se,* but in practice much of the stimulus to the domestic mining industry was exercised via the stockpiling program. Contracts with the federal government to supply stockpile materials at above-market prices were what induced many marginal U.S. metals producers to expand their operations in the early 1950s.

The stockpile in this sense substituted for tariff protection of the domestic mining industry. In his statement announcing expansion of stockpile purchases, President Eisenhower explicitly stated that he had decided against imposing new import tariffs on metals and ores, but that the stockpile purchases were another way to "strengthen and protect our domestic mobilization base."[5]

CIVILIAN OR MILITARY CONTROL?

The passage of the Defense Production Act was evidence that civilian and/or executive-branch agencies were increasingly taking charge of policies concerning domestic military mobilization. President Eisenhower took this trend a step further in 1953 by transferring responsibility for the stockpile from the War Department and Navy Department to a civilian agency, the General Services Administration. This was at least partly in response to the recommendation of the president's commission on Materials Policy (known as the Paley Commission), in its 1952 final report, that the precise duties and relationships among the approximately thirty-eight different agencies and government branches then responsible for various stockpiling operations be clarified.[6]

Eisenhower also deposited surplus Korean War supplies in the stockpile rather than selling them, despite the fact that the stockpile objectives for some of the materials (such as lead and zinc) had already been reached. Moreover, he established new "long-term" procurement goals for some domestically produced metals, which went beyond the regular stockpile goals. These policies were designed to help the U.S. mining industry, but they were viewed with a jaundiced eye by military officials, who regarded especially the "long-term" program as "essentially a 'political' program masquerading as a national security measure and competing for appropriations with higher priority military programs."[7]

This points up a second major debate concerning stockpile policy—between the military, traditionally insistent that the stockpile be used purely for national security purposes, and other policy makers and politicians who were more concerned about its domestic impact.[8]

By the early 1950s, it appeared that the Pentagon had basically lost out in this struggle, although the public view of the stockpile as primarily a military endeavor persisted. In the late 1980s, the Reagan administration again transferred control over the stockpile to the Defense Department, indicating a renewed desire to assert the military nature of the stockpile.

DOMESTIC OR FOREIGN POLICY?

Besides the Defense Production Act, another piece of legislation enacted in the 1950s significantly affected the stockpiling program. This was the Agricultural Trade Development and Assistance Act of 1954, which provided that surplus U.S. agricultural commodities (which had been accumulated to support farm prices) should be bartered for less perishable commodities (such as metals and ores for the stockpile). The U.S. farm surplus products had to be *exported* under the terms of this act, so in practice most of the goods received in return were foreign-produced. The program was administered by the Commodity Credit Corporation, within the Department of Agriculture, via contracts with private U.S. commodity brokers who arranged the trades of U.S. wheat, wool, corn, and other products for foreign-produced commodities. The commodities obtained in this barter process which were needed in the strategic stockpile were transferred into it; if the strategic stockpile objective for a given commodity had already been reached, the material was kept by the Agriculture Department in a "supplemental stockpile."

Two other U.S. laws further affected the stockpile in the same period: the Economic Cooperation Act of 1948 and the Mutual Security Act of 1951. These laws provided that the United States would purchase materials for the stockpile from "participating" foreign countries, and that funds would be provided to these countries to help "promote ... an increase in the production in such participating countr(ies) of materials which are required by the United States as a result of deficiencies or potential deficiencies in the resources within the United States."[9]

Under these programs, U.S.-owned "counterpart funds" (foreign currencies) were reinvested in their home countries for transportation, energy, or mining development projects, and loans repayable in strategic commodities were made for the same purposes.[10] The program financed two geological surveys and a cobalt project in Portuguese and British African colonies, spending a total of $2.1 million on these projects.[11]

FREE MARKET OR MARKET INTERVENTION?

In sum, the U.S. stockpiles were built up in the late 1940s and 1950s through a complex series of domestic and foreign minerals purchase programs, most of which had several political purposes. Contradictions and tensions have been apparent throughout the history of the stockpile along several axes: those between domestic and foreign policy objectives, civilian and military uses of the stockpile, and the extent to which the stockpile should be used to bolster U.S. metals production. These conflicts can be viewed as falling into a familiar pattern in U.S. political debates: how much government intervention in the economy is warranted or desirable?

The "free market" view can be generalized as follows: The stockpile's purpose is to compensate for insufficient U.S. supplies of certain metals. These should therefore be purchased as cheaply as possible from their foreign producers and held for possible use in wartime, in order to strengthen the immediate military capabilities of the United States in the event of a sudden conflict. Control of the stockpile should remain firmly in the hands of the defense establishment. Besides maintaining the necessary stocks of certain strategic commodities which are not produced in the U.S., the stockpile should intervene in the markets for these commodities as little as possible.

An alternate position, which can be characterized as the "market intervention" view, would hold that strategic intervention in metals markets serves U.S. interests best. In this view, stockpile purchases should be used to stimulate domestic production of as many strategic commodities as possible, so that U.S. supplies will be available and long-term production capacities will be in place in the event of military need. Even for foreign-produced commodities, the capacity stimulation provided by stockpile purchases serves to lessen the chances of restricted supply in the future. Government intervention in strategic markets is an inevitable and necessary component of U.S. defense. Moreover, such intervention heightens the political acceptability of military expenditures by concentrating their benefits within the United States, insofar as possible. Control of the stockpile should rest with Congress or the Interior Department.

These extreme positions are meant as a general template for understanding specific debates in stockpile policy. Clearly, in each detailed instance, the interrelationships between interested parties and the views they hold are usually quite complex. But the point remains that stockpile policy represents one aspect of a long and continuing debate in the United States regarding government intervention in markets, and the extent to which "strategic" considerations justify exceptions to normal principles.

NOTES

1. James A. McClure, "Stockpiling of Strategic and Critical Materials," *Idaho Law Review* 19 (1983): 417–53.

2. Section 3(a)(2) of the 1946 Act refers to title III of the Act of March 3, 1933 (47 Stat. 1520), which states, "Unless the head of the department of independent establishment concerned shall determine it to be inconsistent with the public interest, or the cost to be unreasonable, only such ... materials and supplies as have been mined or produced in the United States ... shall be acquired for public use." Quoted in McClure, 419.

3. McClure, 426.

4. Ibid., 428. See also J. D. Morgan, *Strategic Minerals Overview*, unpublished paper presented at the Foreign Service Institute, Science Symposium, 4 March 1981; quoted in Ewan W. Anderson, *The Structure and Dynamics of U.S. Government Policymaking: The Case of Strategic Minerals* (New York: Praeger, 1988), 38.

5. U.S. Congress, Senate, Select Committee on Small Business, Subcommittee No. 2. *Hearings: Problems Resulting from the Exclusion of Small Business from Stockpile Purchases and from Participation in the Disposal of Surplus Products Program*. 84th Congress, 2nd session, July 11, 12, and 17, 1956, 134. See also U.S. Congress, Senate, Committee on Interior and Insular Affairs, Subcommittee on Minerals, Materials, and Fuels. *Hearings: Extension of Purchase Programs of Strategic and Critical Minerals*. 84th Congress, 2nd session, April 19, 20, 21, 25, May 16, 24, and 25, 1956, 29.

6. Anderson, *The Structure and Dynamics of U.S. Government Policymaking*, 41.

7. McClure, 437–38.

8. Ibid., 435.

9. U.S. Congress, Senate, Committee on Interior and Insular Affairs, Subcommittee on Minerals, Materials, and Fuels. *Hearings: Extension of Purchase Programs of Strategic and Critical Minerals*. 84th Congress, 2nd session, April 19, 20, 21, 25, May 16, 24, and 25, 1956, 241–43.

10. Ibid., 242–43.

11. Ibid., 243. Tables showing expenditures under these programs by country and by commodity are given in Ibid., 245–46.

4

Stockpile Surpluses

By the late 1950s, purchases had proceeded to the point that stockpile objectives for many commodities had been met. Several major policy shifts followed, which substantially affected the relationship between stockpile objectives and inventories.

SHIFTS IN OVERALL STOCKPILE POLICY

Stockpile planning from 1946 until 1958 was based on meeting the U.S. economy's needs during a "national emergency" of five years' duration. In 1958, the "five-year" scenario was changed to a "three-year" one, on the rationale that, in the postnuclear age, a long-lasting conflict like World War II was unlikely. The drastic reduction of stockpile objectives meant that large amounts of many stockpiled commodities became surplus. Because of its legal mandate to avoid market disruption, however, the GSA was slow to begin selling these surplus commodities.

President Kennedy ordered an investigation into the stockpiling program in 1962, stating in part:

It was apparent to me that this excessive storage of costly materials was a questionable burden on public funds, and in addition a potential source of excessive and unconscionable profits.... The cloak of secrecy which has surrounded this program may have been justified originally to conceal our shortages, but this is no longer the case, and secrecy now is only an invitation to mismanagement.[1]

As a result of the investigation, conducted by Senator Stuart Symington, information about the stockpile became more readily available, and stockpile objectives were further reduced (to zero, in the case of domestically produced lead and zinc). The stockpile planning assumption that no stockpiled materials would be available from outside of North America during an all-out war was replaced by more moderate assumptions positing some long-distance importing.[2]

As in most cases of stockpile policy changes, there were charges that the Symington investigation was launched for political reasons—either to cast the policies of the Republican Eisenhower administration in a suspicious light, or to "neutralize the political effects of the Billy Sol Estes swindle case in Texas, with its intimation of corruption in the farm-surplus program."[3]

In any case, by 1965, about 60 percent of the stockpile was surplus and subject to disposal, with most of the excess concentrated in twelve materials: aluminum, chromite, cobalt, copper, lead, manganese, molybdenum, nickel, rubber, tin, tungsten, and zinc. The metals on this list are the most important nonferrous industrial metals by value of U.S. consumption (see Table 4.1). As these metals were stockpiled in large quantities owing to their economic importance for the United States, it is not surprising that stockpile surpluses were concentrated in these metals once objectives were lowered in the 1950s and 1960s.

In 1972 President Nixon reduced stockpile objectives still further, basing them on a one-year supply for the U.S. economy. The Nixon goal reduction was made on the recommendation of the National Security Council (NSC), but in announcing it Nixon cited both economic justifications—the inflation-fighting value of keeping commodity prices low by selling stockpiled supplies—and defense-related ones—the NSC's determination that a long war was unlikely and that the economy could fully respond to defense production needs within a year's time.[4]

Balancing the national budget seems also to have been an important factor in Nixon's decision. In subsequent Congressional testimony, S. D. Strauss, vice president of the metal firm ASARCO and representative of the American Mining Congress, stated, "It was widely believed by the business and financial community that this was a major consideration in the decision to virtually liquidate the stockpile."[5]

A stockpiling study prepared for Congress in the mid-1970s saw the Vietnam War as a primary factor in the evolution toward "economic" uses of the stockpile.

In retrospect, the decade of the 1960's was marked by the role played by the national stockpile in dealing with some of the economic consequences of the Vietnam War. When a high level of economic activity coincided with burgeoning requirements for the production of military equipment, materials shortages and upward pressure on prices were the inevitable result. [Defense contractors] ... possessed priority authority in the purchase of materials.... As a consequence, shortage ... impacted entirely on the nonmilitary industrial and civilian economy.... Stockpile sales were made to soften the adverse impact and reduce upward pressure on prices of industrial materials. In some measure, stockpile sales were used to reduce demands for the imposition of wartime material and production controls ...[two-thirds of all sales for the 10-year period 1960-70 took place between 1965 and 1967], which marked the high years of materials requirements related to ... the Vietnam War.... In short, government policy had evolved to the point where the stockpile was being used as a tool for economic stabilization.[6]

The three-year war scenario was reinstated in 1973 to set the parameters for the overall size of stockpile objectives, and this was reiterated by the Reagan admin-

Table 4.1
Comparisons of 1947, 1971, and 1993 Rankings of Metals by Market Value of U.S. Consumption (Excluding Iron Ore, Pig Iron, Gold, Silver, Platinum Group, Uranium, and Vanadium)

1947 Rank Ordering	1971 Rank Ordering	1993 Rank Ordering
Copper*	Aluminum*	Aluminum*
Lead*	Copper*	Copper*
Aluminum*	Zinc*	Titanium (rutile)
Zinc*	Lead*	Zinc*
Manganese*	Nickel*	Lead*
Tin*	Tin*	Nickel*
Nickel*	Manganese*	Cadmium
Chromium*	Bauxite*	Tin*
Bauxite*	Molybdenum*	Cobalt*
Cadmium	Magnesium	Molybdenum*
Antimony	Rutile	Antimony
Molybdenum*	Chromium*	Bauxite and alumina*
Cobalt*	Titanium	Chromium*
Mercury	Cobalt*	Manganese*
Magnesium	Cadmium	Tungsten
Rutile	Antimony	(Mercury not ranked)
Tungsten	Mercury	
(Titanium and	Graphite	
Graphite not ranked)	Tungsten	

Source: Calculated from data in U.S. Department of Commerce, Bureau of the Census, *Statistical Abstract of the United States 1994* (Washington, D.C.: USGPO, 1994), 710.
  U.S. Bureau of Mines, *Minerals Yearbook*, 1947, 1971, and 1993.

* Denotes metals included in this study.

istration in 1982. By 1992, however, the Department of Defense was planning to again drastically reduce its estimate of the length of a conflict for which the stockpile was intended to provide.

Senator Harry Byrd, in a 1981 Congressional hearing, commented with some chagrin:

Since World War II, our stockpile requirement has been a yo-yo. Following World War II, the stockpile requirement was based on anticipated usage for a 5-year war. The 5 was changed to 3, where it is today. At no time were requirements met.

After 60 years of talking about the problem and 40 years of Federal legislation, the stockpile is a mountain of overages and shortages.[7]

MARKET EFFECTS

President Nixon's statement of the rationale behind stockpile goal revisions marked the first official admission of the stockpile's economic potential, although the language of the 1946 law creating it, which forbade it to be used for any purpose other than national defense, began to seem especially naïve in the post-OPEC years. Even the director of the Federal Preparedness Agency, General Leslie Bray, conceded to a Congressional committee in 1976 that budgetary and economic considerations must necessarily play some part in decisions concerning the stockpile. Obviously, economic and military activities have been closely connected in the United States since well before World War II, so the distinction between "defense-related" and "non-defense-related" justifications for stockpile transactions is at best a question of semantics and at worst a politically useful smokescreen.

Also naïve, at least in hindsight, was the law's requirement that the GSA attempt to keep stockpile transactions from disrupting world markets. Since for most of the commodities in the stockpile, the United States is the world's largest consumer, a stockpile inventory representing a five-year supply for the U.S. might represent a quantity more than equivalent to a year's total world production (see Table 1.3, chapter 1). By 1972, up to four-fifths of this stock had been deemed "excess" by the U.S. government (that is, unnecessary for defense purposes), and thus available to be sold at any time. In fact, after the late 1950s, the GSA was constantly in the position of an actual or potential seller on the world market for many metals. As the case studies in this volume make clear, this had the effect of dampening price increases and, in some cases, helping to depress markets for a number of stockpiled commodities.

Despite these market effects, U.S. government policy statements about the stockpile endeavored to downplay its potential for planned market intervention. The Strategic and Critical Materials Stock Piling Revision Act of 1979, for example, contains the following provision: "Stockpiles are for the purpose of the common defense of the United States, not as a means of controlling or influencing commodity prices."

The most recent amendments to the stockpile legislation continue to include a similar statement, which has been a part of the stockpile acts throughout their history: "The purpose of the National Defense Stockpile is to serve the interest of national defense only. The National Defense Stockpile is not to be used for economic or budgetary purposes."[8]

Following revisions to the Stockpiling Act in 1979, which created the National Defense Stockpile Transaction Fund, proceeds from sales of stockpiled commodities were set aside to be spent (with specific Congressional approval) on acquisitions of other materials for the stockpile. A controversial ruling in 1982 that this stockpile transaction fund was a "revolving fund" clarified that this did not remove stockpile assets from the general U.S. government budget; it did, however, somewhat reduce the political pressure to sell off stockpile materials as a budget-balancing tactic, since the proceeds could not be used for nonstockpile purposes.[9]

Stockpile acquisitions basically ended for twenty years in July 1958, and from then until 1973, excess materials were slowly sold off. At least in part because of concerns about market effects, a large disposal of "surplus" stockpile materials planned for 1973 was called off, and no further sales were made until December 1979. The Reagan administration announced its intention to purchase aluminum and cobalt for the stockpile in 1981, as part of a new emphasis on strategic materials and military preparedness. Sales of other stockpile commodities announced at the same time were blocked in Congress for years,[10] but between 1979 and 1985, about $429 million worth of surplus materials were sold and another $368 million was spent on new acquisitions for the stockpile.[11]

The stockpile was the major issue addressed in the 1982 *National Materials and Minerals Program Plan and Report to Congress*, prepared by a Cabinet committee. In addition to calling for a comprehensive review of stockpile requirements, the Program Plan provided more guidance to the GSA than prior stockpile policy statements regarding how the stockpile was to be managed. It recommended a five-year planning process for GSA acquisitions and disposals, and fiscal year plans that would incorporate "annual budget ceilings, market conditions, immediate strategic requirements, and GSA purchase activities." On the question of whether the stockpile itself or stimulus of domestic metals industries was more central to meeting U.S. defense needs, the Program Plan straddled the fence:

The Administration will rely primarily on the strategic stockpile as the primary means of providing for national defense objectives. However, analysis is now ongoing to determine whether circumstances exist under which the use of Defense Production Act incentives would be more cost-effective than stockpile purchases.[12]

The close relationship between stockpile policy and other forms of government support for national industries is clear, but the stockpile's actions have had many other types of effects as well. The following chapters focus on some of these influences.

NOTES

1. James A. McClure, "Stockpiling of Strategic and Critical Materials," *Idaho Law Review* 19 (1983): 446–47.

2. Ibid., 447.

3. Ibid., 448.

4. U.S. Congress, Joint Committee on Banking. *Hearings: Defense Industrial Base. Part 3: New Stockpile Objectives.* 94th Congress, 2nd session, November 24, 1976, 38. Nixon's message to Congress proposing the new stockpile legislation stated: "Short-term demand for many commodities has outpaced short-term supplies. As a result, prices for industrial commodities have recently been increasing at unacceptably high rates—in

some cases by more than 30 percent in the last 12 months alone. These increases will eventually be felt in higher prices for the American consumer if we do not act decisively now. By disposing of unneeded items in the strategic stockpile, we can strike a critical blow for the American consumer." Nixon asked for omnibus disposal authorization from Congress to sell sixteen different commodities, to avoid the usual delays in obtaining Congressional approval on a commodity-by-commodity basis for proposed sales. See U.S. Congress, *Message from the President of the United States—Disposal of Various Materials from the National Stockpile*, April 16, 1973.

5. U.S. Congress, House of Representatives, Armed Services Committee, Subcommittee on Seapower and Strategic and Critical Materials. *Hearings on H.R. 15081*. 94th Congress, 2nd session, August 26 and September 1, 1976, 5.

6. U.S. Congress, *Assessment of Alternative Stockpiling Policies*. Report prepared for the House Science and Technology Committee. 94th Congress, 2nd session, August, 1976, 238–39.

7. *Congressional Record*. 97th Congress, 1st session, 1981, Vol. 127, pt. 34; cited in Anderson, 79.

8. Cited in U.S. Department of Defense, *Strategic and Critical Materials Report to the Congress: Operations under the Strategic and Critical Materials Stock Piling Act during the Period April 1991–September 1991*, April 1992, 17.

9. Anderson, 51–52, 67.

10. Anderson, 51, 57.

11. Anderson, 87.

12. Program Plan, 17; quoted in Anderson, 58.

Part II

Stockpile Policy and Market Effects

The following two chapters discuss themes that are important in the making of stockpile policy and its effects on metal markets. These include the role of various domestic political factors within the United States and "pork barrel" politics, foreign policy factors, the interrelationship between Congress, the President, and the Defense Department, and even the efforts of the GSA not to disrupt markets. Questions of how to assess the importance of the stockpile in metals price determination are then addressed.

5

Political Influence, Foreign Policy, and the Stockpile

Throughout the various changes in stockpile objectives and overall policy, political factors relating to both domestic and foreign policy seem to have fairly consistently outweighed national security considerations. This is clearly revealed in transcripts of Congressional hearings concerning the stockpile.[1]

DOMESTIC POLITICAL FACTORS

During a 1976 Congressional hearing, Senator William Proxmire closely questioned the director of the Federal Preparedness Agency, General Leslie Bray, regarding non-defense-related influences on the stockpile's administration. "If a close friend of the administration wishes to have a material bought in which he has a financial interest, why couldn't this easily be done with little or no accountability?" Proxmire wondered. "How about ... industry coming on hands and knees, perhaps saying we need some help, we need to have you stabilize our prices or keep our price from falling, or maybe increase our price for various reasons? What is there to prevent that kind of action which I think is subject to extremely dangerous corruption?" "Yes, sir," answered General Bray. "I am very sensitive to that.... Now, it is not possible for me to go back and say whether or not there were economic uses at different times during ... history ... I am sure in the past history there have always been those different views by different segments of industry, some opposed to releases, some advocating releases. My point is the decision should be made, though, on the necessity of the release for the common defense, for our national security interest, and only that. The only thing I can assure you is that the law says that, and as long as I am director of the Federal Preparedness Agency, any recommendation I make to a President would strongly emphasize that particular point."[2]

Later in the hearing Bray stated that investigations of GSA actions affecting various different commodities—aluminum, tin, chromium, diamonds, and copper—had turned up no sign of undue pressure from special interest groups,[3] and he gave similar assurances that inflation control,[4] budget effects,[5] desire to break producer cartels,[6] and international political and foreign policy considerations[7] were not considered in reaching stockpile goals. Senator Proxmire countered:

Now, General Bray, given a very substantial increase in the stockpile goals, even over the pre-1973 levels, it is hard to avoid the conclusion that they serve some purpose other than the national defense, either that or the people formerly in charge of the stockpiles were negligent or didn't understand stockpiles, for example. It is well known that Secretary (of State) Kissinger favors a policy of stabilizing prices and markets to prevent cartels in producing nations. What assurances do we have that the stockpile goals are not aimed at world price and market stabilization?

General Bray responded stolidly, "I do not agree that our new goals reflect any change in intent in the use of the stockpile beyond those very narrow purposes of the Strategic and Critical Materials Stock Piling Act."[8]

Senator Proxmire's concern about opportunities for corruption in stockpile dealings was perhaps counterbalanced by the following input from Senator Strom Thurmond in another hearing:

THURMOND: Did the administration consult with industry representatives as to the economic impact of the disposal recommendations?

SEBASTIAN J. GIUFRIDDA, GSA ECONOMIST: Senator, we are in constant touch with the markets on especially the major items, and we have a very good feel of what will disrupt a market and what will not. Does that answer your question?

THURMOND: No, it doesn't. You may have the feel, but I want to know, did you get the opinion of industry on these matters and what impact they felt it would have on the disposal recommendations?

GIUFRIDDA: We discussed with the Department of Commerce, which has direct contact with the consumers.... We, as I say, have a good feel of what is in the [industry's] judgement disruptive.

THURMOND: You are saying you have a good feel of it. That is your opinion. You might be wrong. Isn't it worthwhile to consult with the industry, with some of the leaders of this Nation, the businessmen who helped to make this country great, isn't it worthwhile to get their opinions—whether you follow them or not—as to what impact your disposal recommendations will have?[9]

Even if the "national defense" was quite honestly the major consideration for decision makers, there could of course be honest differences of opinion among Congressional, administration, and GSA officials about what constituted the best defense-related stockpile policy. But in any case, various investigators throughout the stockpile's history were clearly (and rightfully) suspicious about the leeway offered by the stockpile for nonstrategic political maneuvring.

Clearly, stockpile policy is no different in principle than other aspects of policy formation within the U.S. government; a number of complex interrelationships among political actors are inevitably involved. These include industry lobbies,[10] transnational corporations,[11] representatives of foreign interests,[12] and personal relationships or political obligations among decision makers. There also may be parallel hierarchies and common interests among bureaucratic, Congressional, and Executive-branch bodies involved in policy making. At different times in its history, the stockpile has been at least partially controlled by all of these types of government agencies.

However, all three are influenced (in varying degrees) by some of the same factors. These include special interest groups, public awareness of and concern with the issue in question, the number of people affected, the expected impact of the issue on the domestic economy, and the degree of interest in the issue held by individuals in key positions for influencing the course of government policy.

This implies that despite the number of domestic agencies and institutions that are involved in stockpile policy making, similar political considerations may be involved for most of them.

A 1980 study specifically designed to test whether the U.S. stockpile has acted like an economic buffer-stock to stabilize metal markets comments that, although the stockpile has clear tendencies in this direction, political factors seem to have intervened to prevent long-term market stabilization by the stockpile.

Operation of the strategic stockpile for market stabilization purposes has seldom persisted on a significant scale for more than two or three years. This is undoubtedly due to both economic and political pressures which build up to curtail stockpiling.

If an economic stockpile is to stabilize a market successfully, it may require a large quantity of material to be either purchased or sold over an extended period. Past U.S. stockpiling activity has been unwilling to follow such a pattern. Additionally, there comes a point when buying or selling more material does not square with the stated purpose of the stockpile, which is for military objectives. Initially this pressure may be weak; however, as excessively large stockpiles are accumulated, or on the other hand practically eliminated, members of Congress and industry become more concerned with the impacts of stockpiling and try to stop government market intervention. This combination of the necessity to meet strategic considerations along with the possible need of long term market intervention has ultimately inhibited the government from carrying buffer stock operations to a logical conclusion.[13]

This study, which focuses on the markets for tin, lead, and zinc, concludes that the strategic stockpile may help to stabilize markets for a year or two, but that it also shifts short-run supply and demand curves in a manner that often is ultimately destabilizing. This is because "pressures to maintain the stockpiles at militarily acceptable levels, as well as the possible need to intervene in the market on an extended basis, prevents the government from carrying out economic stockpiling for more than several years."[14]

FOREIGN POLICY

Although General Bray in his 1976 testimony denied that foreign policy considerations played any role in stockpile decision making, GSA officials responded somewhat differently to Congressional questions about this by 1979—as in this interchange between Senator Gary Hart, chairman of the Armed Services committee's subcommittee on Military Construction and Stockpiles, and Paul Krueger, a GSA official:

HART: Let me ask about the foreign policy considerations involved here and how they get factored into your commodity proposals. I am referring specifically to the situation in Bolivia, that country's dependence on the world tin market. We will have testimony later, sponsored by the Bolivian Embassy and human rights groups, that calls the tin disposal into question. Was the Bolivian tin question addressed in arriving at your proposal? What role did foreign policy considerations play?

KRUEGER: The interagency group which comes up with the annual materials plan consists of four subcommittees. One of these subcommittees addresses international considerations and is chaired by the Department of State with participation by the Department of Defense, Federal Preparedness Agency, and the Department of Commerce. The purpose of that subcommittee is, in particular, to look at not only domestic market impact but what are the international impacts of these commodity transactions since many of these markets are, in fact, international markets. So it is within that forum that the international policy considerations as well as international economic impacts are considered.[15]

A State Department representative also stated in the same hearing that foreign policy and international economic factors should certainly be considered in stockpile planning.[16] Senator Hart, later in the hearing, commented on the difficulty of including foreign policy concerns in decisions concerning the stockpile:

Let me just say that it is unfortunate that we cannot calculate in dollar terms the importance to this country of a democratic Bolivia with a sound economy. That would make it easier for us to weigh these considerations. I am hopeful that this committee and the administration will constantly keep in mind that the goal of a stable Bolivia is a very important one for us and in our interest.[17]

By 1980, the State Department was soliciting views of more than thirty countries before deciding on its recommendations concerning stockpile disposals.[18]

Whether foreign policy considerations played a *de facto* role in stockpile policy (despite GSA officials' denials) in the pre-1971 period is difficult to determine, although the barter and aid components of some stockpile acquisition programs clearly had foreign policy implications.

Foreign policy considerations are probably of less significance in U.S. government decision making than domestically related factors. However, as Anderson notes in a thorough examination of the external aspects of U.S. government strategic materials policy, "Since most trade in strategic minerals must, by definition, be international, vulnerability immediately becomes a foreign policy issue."[19] This has been stated quite openly by U.S. government officials; an example is Secretary of State George Shultz's call for using U.S. foreign aid to reflect America's interest in obtaining and protecting free access to important primary resources in other parts of the world.[20]

In some specific cases, as discussed in the case studies in this volume, foreign policy aspects of stockpile policy decisions seem to have been central.

NOTES

1. That both the political nature of stockpile policy making and the awareness of its market effects changed little from the 1940s to the present is attested to by numerous sources, e.g.: Robert A. Cornell, "United States Stockpile Policy," (mimeo), paper presented at the American Mining Congress Mining Convention, Los Angeles, September 23–26, 1979; R. H. Ramsey, "The Snarl in Stockpiling Means Trouble for You," *Engineering and Mining Journal* (September 1949): 72–75; "By All Means ... Let's Have the Facts About Stockpiling," *Engineering and Mining Journal* (March 1962): 4, 73; Frederick J. Dobney, "Stockpiling and Shortages," *Social Science Quarterly* (September 1976): 455–65; Gerald E. Gauntt, "Market Stabilization and the Strategic Stockpile," *Materials and Society* 4 (1980): 203–9; Bruce C. Netschert, "U.S. Dependence on Imported Nonfuel Minerals: The Threat of Mini-OPECs?" *Journal of Metals* (March 1981): 31–38; and U.S. Congress, House of Representatives, Committee on Interior and Insular Affairs, Subcommittee on Mines and Mining, *U.S. Minerals Vulnerability: National Policy Implications.* 96th Congress, 2nd session, November 1980.

2. U.S. Congress, Joint Committee on Banking. *Hearings: Defense Industrial Base. Part 3: New Stockpile Objectives.* 94th Congress, 2nd session, November 24, 1976, 13–14.

3. Ibid., 55.

4. Ibid., 20, 35.

5. Ibid., 11–12.

6. Ibid., 36.

7. Ibid., 33.

8. Ibid., 35–36. See also U.S. Congress, *Assessment of Alternative Stockpiling Policies.* Report prepared for the House Science and Technology Committee. 94th Congress, 2nd session, August 1976, 34–35; U.S. Congress, Senate, Armed Services Committee, Subcommittee on Military Construction and Stockpiles. *Hearings: General Stockpile Policy.* 95th Congress, 1st session, September 9, 1977, 56–58; U.S. Congress, House of Representatives, Armed Services Committee, Subcommittee on Seapower and Strategic and Critical Materials. *Hearings on H.R. 9486, a Bill to Authorize a Contribution by the U.S. to the Tin Buffer Stock Established under the Fifth International Tin Agreement.* 95th Congress, 2nd session, May 15, 1978, 8ff.

9. U.S. Congress, Senate, Armed Services Committee, Subcommittee on Military Construction and Stockpiles. *Hearings: Consideration of Stockpile Legislation.* 95th Congress, 2nd session, March 8 and 9, 1978, 98–99.

10. Lester M. Salamon and J. J. Siegfried, "Economic Power and Political Influence: The Impact of Industry Structure on Public Policy," *American Political Science Review* 71 (1977): 1026–43; Sar A. Levitan and Martha R. Cooper, *Business Lobbies: The Public Good and the Bottom Line* (Baltimore: Johns Hopkins University Press, 1984); Edward

Handler and J. R. Mulkern, *Business in Politics* (Lexington: Lexington Books, 1982); John M. Kline, *State Government Influence in United States International Economic Policy* (Lexington: Lexington Books, 1983); Ernest H. Preeg, *Traders and Diplomats: An Analysis of the Kennedy Round of Negotiations Under the GATT* (Washington: Brookings, 1970); and W. A. Brock and S. P. Magee, "The Economics of Special Interest Politics: The Case of the Tariff," *American Economic Review*, 68, 2 (May 1978): 246–50.

11. G. K. Helleiner, "Transnational Enterprises and the New Political Economy of U.S. Trade Policy," *Oxford Economic Papers* 29, 1 (March 1977): 102–16; and Preeg, 1970.

12. J. S. Odell, "Latin American Trade Negotiations with the U.S." *International Organization* 34 (Spring 1980): 207–28; Stephen D. Krasner, "State Power and the Structure of International Trade," *World Politics* 28, 3 (April 1976): 317–47; and Jonathan Sanford, "Congressional Testimony by Foreign Officials and Citizens," *Library of Congress Study,* reprinted in *Congressional Record* 15 (June 1976): E3346–47.

13. Gerald E. Gauntt, "Market Stabilization and the Strategic Stockpile," 208.

14. Gauntt, 209.

15. U.S. Congress, Senate, Armed Services Committee, Subcommittee on Military Construction and Stockpiles. *Hearing: Stockpile Commodity Legislation.* 96th Congress, 1st session, July 10, 1979, 11.

16. Ibid., 18–21.

17. Ibid., 32.

18. U.S. Congress, House of Representatives, Armed Services Committee, Subcommittee on Seapower and Strategic and Critical Materials. *Hearings: National Defense Stockpile.* 97th Congress, 1st Session, June 2 and 4, 1981, 74.

19. Anderson, 145.

20. N. S. Zank, *The Effect of U.S. Economic Assistance on the Supply of Critical Raw Materials* (Washington: Agency for International Development, 1983), 11; cited in Anderson, 145.

6

The Stockpile and Market Disruption

Speculation about when and how much stockpiled material the GSA would buy or sell initiated waves of price fluctuations throughout the postwar period—most noticeably when Congressional hearings were being held or votes taken on legislation concerning the stockpile.[1]

The stockpile's contribution to market uncertainty was partly due to a certain lack of clarity of GSA internal objectives regarding the stockpile and the means which it felt were acceptable in order to meet those goals.[2] Also contributing to the uncertainty were the possible changes in directives, which could be handed down at any time by the administration, as were President Nixon's in 1973, and which might reflect any of a broad range of considerations, from changes in defense technology or foreign policy to a desire to please certain Senators or taxpayers, or attempts to balance the budget. A further center of uncertainty concerning stockpile policy was Congress' legal oversight of all stockpile purchases and most sales.

It could even be argued that the GSA's mandate not to contribute to market disruptions *itself* had a destabilizing effect, insofar as it contributed to a certain lack of transparency concerning Congressional directives regarding the stockpile, and the process used by the GSA to make its sales or purchases. For example, the GSA was unwilling to make public the list of commodities it intended to request Congressional permission to acquire, partly for fear of causing speculation in those markets.[3] These (not always successful) efforts to keep secret the details of the decision-making process, and sometimes even the decisions themselves, apparently resulted from a belief that this would reduce their market impact. But overall, secrecy and uncertainty surrounding the stockpile and its motives seemingly contributed significantly to market speculation in commodity markets.

The speculation was also partly due to the fact that stockpile transactions were quite often made at prices that differed, sometimes very significantly, from the world market price for the metal in question. This was because the GSA, as mentioned above, sometimes bought metals from U.S. domestic producers at high prices in order to subsidize them; at other times it also was able to work out deals with metals suppliers for below-market rates on the huge government supply contracts. Moreover, when the GSA sold metals, its prices tended to be low— either because buyers would insist on lower prices (due to the low quality of stockpiled stocks being "rotated" or in compensation for the bureaucratic difficulties of dealing with the government), or because subsidizing domestic users of the metals being sold was a political reason for making the sales. As mentioned above, the GSA also, at times, arranged its purchases outside of normal market channels for other buyers—via government-to-government barter negotiations with metals-producing countries, for example.[4]

The U.S. minerals industry has traditionally distrusted stockpiles because of this well-documented contribution to uncertainty. The American Mining Congress, an industry association, has long been on record as favoring the rationalization, or even abolition, of U.S. stockpiles, for this reason. Stated American Mining Congress representative S. D. Strauss at a 1976 Congressional hearing, "The constant shift in stockpile goals ... very accurately described earlier as yo-yo, has caused the stockpile to be an extremely disruptive influence in the markets for metals and minerals, and also it has been expensive to the taxpayer." He termed the stockpile a "sword of Damocles" hanging over the mining industry's head,[5] and added, "I think if you would ask the chief executive officer of almost every major mining company, he would say that from the standpoint of the industry, they would just as soon have no stockpiles at all."[6]

Care must clearly be used in discussing the effect of uncertainty on speculation and the overall market, however. To the extent that futures markets allow risks to be spread, and commodity speculation therefore serves a useful purpose in reducing the violence of price swings by increasing their frequency, it cannot be said that speculation alone is cause for concern. Rather, it is the dominance of one actor in the market which removes most of the objective (as well as financial) rewards of speculation. As one study of the tin market noted:

One of the characteristics favorable to a futures market and the development of lively speculation is the absence of private monopolistic power or discretionary power over price by any other body. Thus ... [U.S.] stockpile liquidations and the buffer stock operations of the International Tin Council have made things difficult at times for the London Metals Exchange. To cite a recent example, in September 1978, at a time when there was a great deal of uncertainty as to the intentions of the U.S. government regarding disposals of tin from the strategic stockpile, the *Wall Street Journal* cited one dealer as noting that "fabricators, merchants and customers are those primarily making the market currently," and quoted another as saying that "speculative interest in the market at the moment is the smallest for many, many years."[7]

Most metal market experts have regarded uncertainty over GSA actions as a prime cause of price variations in the 1960s and 1970s. For example, Helen Hughes writes that although international buffer stocks help to reduce price fluctuations, "national buffer stocks generally maintained for defense purposes, in contrast, have tended to exacerbate price fluctuations." The United Nations, in a 1984 study on price forecasting for minerals and metals, comments that:

Decisions to establish strategic and stabilization stockpiles also have a significant effect on prices. This effect may be dominant in some cases since it may ultimately influence the behaviour of the private participants in the market, a factor which is not often recognized in analyses of commodity price forecasts and stabilization.[8]

With regard to the legal proscription against market effects of the stockpile's operations, GSA official Roy Markon was asked in a 1979 Congressional hearing whether stockpile managers had a rule of thumb or gauge for the quantities of any commodity that could safely be sold without disrupting the market. He replied, "We make an analysis of the entire market, the annual activity in that particular commodity, both nationally and internationally, and project into that market activity our specific amounts. The data we get out of that modeling provide these quantities for us." Another GSA official stated, "I should add that these commodities don't enter the market all at once. They are marketed in much smaller increments than what these [disposal] bills would allow. While this detailed analysis is very useful before the fact, it is when you actually enter the market and assess the reaction of the market to either your acquisition or disposal and see this reaction, you can then pace additional acquisitions and disposals." Markon then stated, "I might add that prior to the development of the annual disposal plan, we meet with industry to consult and get the direct input from particular producers and consumers as to their projected effects of our activity in the market."[9]

What emerges is a picture of somewhat-refined trial and error as the basis for GSA's market disruption determinations. Left unspecified by government officials was what level of market reaction to GSA activity would be deemed acceptable—for as American Mining Congress representative S. D. Strauss stated at another hearing, "The fact remains that every transaction affects the market; every purchase adds to the demand; every sale adds to the supply."

Another stockpile official revealed at a hearing later in 1979 that the GSA tried not to buy or sell more than 10 percent of U.S. consumption of any commodity within a year's time, using this as a rule of thumb for avoiding market disruptions.[10]

In a paper presented at the convention of the American Mining Congress in 1979, the Assistant Commissioner for Stockpile Transactions admitted that revisions in the stockpile's objectives by the early 1970s had led to disgruntlement in the mining industry. "Many thought that the sales program was being overdone, that the methodology by which the planners set the stockpile requirements needed reconsideration, and that the (perfectly legal) procedure of pushing disposals on the basis of lowered strategic requirements came too dangerously close to use of the stockpile for non-defense purposes....," he stated. "On the other side of the ledger, the same effects of time and industrial progress which created the redundancies have opened great deficit gaps between goals and stocks for another 43 commodities on the stockpile list.... The larger deficits tend to be concentrated in a relatively small number of commodities and they could not be eliminated quickly except at the cost of severe market disruption, which is neither wanted nor permitted under the law."[11]

The creation of the stockpile Transactions Fund under the terms of the Stockpile Revision Act (PL 96-41), passed in 1979, would help to minimize market disruptions, according to this GSA official. Because materials could only be purchased for the stockpile with proceeds from the sale of other materials, "the stockpile managers must sell dear and buy cheap—and that is, in fact, an injunction calculated to stabilize rather than disrupt the commodities markets in which they will deal. The Government will be in there selling when everybody else is buying, and buying when all the world is selling, or wishing it could."[12]

Another change in stockpile administrative procedures resulting from the 1979 law was also expected to reduce market influences resulting from stockpile acquisitions or sales at nonmarket prices, which the GSA official referred to rather obliquely in his speech to the American Mining Congress:

FPRS [the Federal Property Resources Service of the GSA] also has gotten its operating policies and priorities in order. Following the guidance of the [1979] law, the use of competitive methods of sale and purchase will be stressed to the limit, and any deviations from this rule will have to be not only well-justified as a matter of good business economics and sound public policy but also reported in full detail to the Congress. At the same time, a thorough review is underway of the performance standards and provisions built into all stockpile transactions contracts, to make sure that they are up to date, conformed with current commercial practice, and responsive to Federal contracting law and regulations.[13]

The stockpile's overall market effects promised to be substantially reduced by the terms of the 1979 law stated this GSA official, repeatedly assuring his American Mining Congress audience that the GSA did not wish to disrupt markets:

Those in the Government who are concerned with stockpile matters are not insensitive to the damage that unwise GSA operations could do to the markets. There can be no compromise with the principle of responsible, non-disruptive market activity. In this context, P.L. 96-41 and the policies that have been designed around it offer high hopes for progress toward effectively restructuring the stockpile to meet the nation's critical needs for strategic materials in time of war.[14]

While it is clear that the GSA has generally made attempts to reduce the short-term market impact of its sales, long-term effects of stockpile transactions are unavoidable because of their effects on both demand and supply in metal markets. Anderson has noted the "evidence to suggest that the presence of a National Defense Stockpile militates against private sector stockpiling of various kinds," and he also comments that stockpile transactions probably have a larger effect on markets than other forms of government intervention such as regulatory reform, changes in resource availability, or research and development expenditures.[15]

Anderson goes on to remark, in connection with stockpile policy in the 1980s:

[I]t must be remembered that each GSA transaction is unique, and the problems posed by each commodity are different. Also, in the interest of goodwill, great pains are taken to avoid undue disruption. Each activity is effectively *ad hoc* in nature and does not form part of a general policy which, in any case, would be extremely difficult to fashion. Broadly speaking, the GSA adopts a low profile and follows the market, completing transactions in small increments. The result is that the perceptions engendered by potential transactions may be far worse than the actual event.[16]

In the light of evidence presented in the case studies in this volume, Anderson's assessment seems rather sanguine. Absence of a clearly articulated policy involving use of the stockpile to keep resource prices low does not necessarily mean that this is not part of the complex political calculus surrounding stockpile policy. In any event, the effects on metal markets are the same, whether or not they result from purposeful action on the part of stockpile managers and policy makers; and as any futures speculator knows, "perceptions" can be just as important as more concrete effects.

Appendix C to this volume contains a preliminary econometric assessment of the stockpile's price effects in a number of important metal markets. Its results confirm that the stockpile has indeed had an important influence in individual markets and on metals prices in general in the post–World War II period.

METAL MARKET MODELS IN ASSESSING MARKET EFFECTS OF THE STOCKPILE

Metal markets obviously vary greatly among each other and over time in terms of market structure, the substitutability and complementarity of other metals for various uses, the speed and specifics of technological change, and the political and resource-based constraints on the metal's availability. Models of many different types have been employed for various purposes related to analysis of metal markets. In a 1984 report, the United Nations Department of International Economic and Social Affairs categorizes these different modeling techniques as follows: Qualitative methods, cost and reserve-based methods, trend extrapolation, time-series methods, econometric market models, reduced-form methods, and global model systems. The report notes that each of these approaches has characteristics that make it more appropriate for some purposes but not others. For assessing feedbacks in metal markets and for policy analysis, econometric modeling is one of the best techniques.[17] Some authors have also pointed out that composite models using econometric information supplemented with data from time series, futures markets, experts' opinions, and other information may be even more useful in commodity market modeling than any of these alone. A shortcoming of econometric models is that they cannot predict political events, which often have major effects on metal markets.[18]

The tendency in the literature on econometric models of metal markets is toward ever more precision and detail in model specification. Since the early 1970s, many such models have been built privately, for use in predicting future price trends (or even for advising the GSA on how to manage the strategic stockpile). The most current of these models are not in the public domain, since their builders—consulting firms such as Wharton Econometrics and Charles River Associates—use them in their forecasting work for paying clients. Thus, the "state of the art" in terms of detailed econometric models of metal markets is no longer (if it ever was) in the academic realm.[19]

There are, however, substantial doubts on the part of some experts about the ability of even quite detailed econometric models to provide satisfactory price explanations or predictions. Greater model size and complexity does not necessarily imply significantly greater forecasting ability. This may be due to the vulnerability of metals markets to a wide range of external influences, and the difficulties inherent in including accurate estimations of all of them in the models. These potential influences include technological breakthroughs, substitution effects between and among metals, recycling, environmental and resource use policies of governments, the behavior of publicly and privately held stocks and international buffer stocks, speculation, market cornering attempts, cartel formation, international trade and commodity agreements, strikes and political change in both producing and consuming areas, interest rates, and energy prices.[20]

Moreover, as one recent study emphasizes, price formation in minerals markets is determined not only by market conditions (e.g., supply and demand factors), but also by market structure (i.e., the configuration of market actors and their relative power), and the implications of market structure for bargaining and the division of gains from trade. The price actually paid for metals often differs from published "producer prices" or prices on metal exchanges by a premium, which may vary for each individual transaction depending on transport costs, convenience, and other undefined factors. Accurate price modeling, especially in monopolistic or oligopolistic markets, can be quite difficult in the face of theory and data limitations. Humility and caution are called for in interpreting the results of modeling exercises.[21]

Despite these recognized difficulties, hundreds of attempts have been made to model specific metal markets, mostly for the purpose of price forecasting but also to predict demand, analyze changes in market structure, and explore the process of technological change.[22] These models vary widely in their details and specifications, and results are often fairly sensitive to how market characteristics, such as stock mechanisms, are modeled.[23]

As evidenced by these models, econometric market modeling usually consists of modeling supply and demand and inventory behavior, along with their roles in determining price. Price, in conjunction with exogenous variables, affects the supply, demand, and stock variables, which in turn determine the equilibrium price and quantity. The different models are distinguished by the technological and institutional variables relevant to each particular industry, or by their emphasis on particular market forces or the behavior of specific decision makers.[24]

Appendix B summarizes the structure of a number of market models for metals included in this study and lists the variables that they incorporate. Several general comments about these models are in order. First, a basic competitive supply and demand structure is nearly always assumed, despite the fact that most metal industries are quite concentrated and/or vertically integrated. (Concentration ratios have generally been falling since World War II, but they are still high in most metal industries.)

Second, price has been found to be insignificant in the determination of both demand and supply for some metals (e.g., tin and zinc); also prices sometimes do not appear to clear the market, and/or two or more different prices exist simultaneously (e.g., tin, aluminum, zinc, and copper). Third, market modelers have noted difficulties with representing stocks/inventories and the widely differing production techniques which are used simultaneously in some industries (e.g., tin).

The following sections discuss several existing metal market models in more detail, especially with regard to their representations of the effects of the strategic stockpile. Many of the published models of metal markets include the U.S. stockpile as a factor, in some capacity. Often the stockpile is employed as an instrumental variable in the price equation. Successive iterations to achieve a price equation with a good fit in these models generally show the stockpile as an important variable. The models are discussed below in alphabetical order by metal.

ALUMINUM AND BAUXITE

Woods and Burrows' study of bauxite/aluminum[25] discusses the vertical integration of the industry, with price changing infrequently and the six firms in the industry usually following a price leader. From 1947 to 1956 in the United States, the price was too low to clear the market, as a result of government intervention, and supplier allocations/rationing was the result, in addition to much use of secondary aluminum and recycling. The price of secondary metal actually rose well above that of primary aluminum for several years. From 1956 to 1965 and after 1970, the primary aluminum price set by the industry was too high to clear the market and there was overcapacity in production.

The Woods-Burrows model thus contains two prices—list price and transactions price—and consists of a demand equation and the two price equations (which include supply factors such as total capacity, along with other variables).

The authors point out that "the price equations in effect serve the function of defining supply behavior." The best list price equation estimated (over the period 1948–1973) sets price as a function of the cost of producing primary aluminum, plus a dummy variable for 1953–1957 and another for 1972–1973 (because of government interventions in the market in those years). A variable for U.S. stockpile purchases was also tested but not found to be significant, as was another variable for shipments for defense applications. "The[se] two variables were tested on the theory that as government purchases of aluminum are less elastic with respect to price than industrial demand, an increase in these shipments not only would increase the total market for aluminum but would reduce the price elasticity of aggregate demand, resulting in an increase in the industry's desired price." As mentioned, this was not borne out.

CHROMIUM

A study undertaken in 1981 for the U.S. Bureau of Mines to test different policy responses to chromium shortages focused specifically on releases from the strategic stockpile. It used a model that apparently combined political assessments, an interindustry analysis, and an econometric market forecasting model involving supply-and-demand functions, historical data, and "likely producer and consumer responses to disruptive conditions." The modelers make various assumptions regarding stockpile releases in the event that chromium supplies from South Africa are disrupted,[26] and they examine whether stockpile releases, a guaranteed U.S. minimum price for domestic chromium production, or a combination of the two policies would best deal with U.S. vulnerability to a chromium supply disruption. They conclude that stockpile releases generally represent the best policy option. Unfortunately, little detail is provided regarding the form or specification of the quantitative models used; however, it is clear that political and qualitative analysis is a large part of the study.

COBALT

Burrows' cobalt market model[27] takes account of the oligopolistic nature of the cobalt supply situation by hypothesizing a demand function, assuming price is set by the one dominant firm to maximize its total revenue, and then deriving the total suppliers' offer curve—which can be used along with the demand curve to predict future price. In estimating the model, Burrows uses an instrumental variables approach because correlation between Quantity Demanded and the error term in the Demand equation would mean that the Ordinary Least Squares estimation technique would be biased and inconsistent. The equations that give the best results show the price of cobalt as a function of total U.S. industrial consumption of cobalt, U.S. government stocks of cobalt, U.S. government net purchases of cobalt, and dummy variables to capture shifts in demand for technological reasons.[28]

Adams, in another model of the cobalt market,[29] assumes that the production of Zaire (the dominant producer) is equal to world consumption minus whatever cobalt is supplied by other smaller producers, and that Zaire sets the price in relation to the share of other countries' production, and U.S. (mainly government stockpile) stock changes, in world consumption. Demand and price are independent and simultaneously determined; production outside Zaire is independent of this; Zaire's production is determined as a residual but is indirectly dependent on price through consumption. This model predicts price very well for the period 1957–1969. U.S. stock changes are thus a key element in price formation.

COPPER

Wagenhals' copper model[30] estimates supply and demand equations—which he calls "mine production capacity" and "consumption plus storage," respectively—for each of the major producing and consuming countries over the period 1956–1980. The U.S. stockpile is included on the demand side, as a component of "storage." The government stockpile is not mentioned on the supply side, nor are non-market-price stockpile transactions. Wagenhals does go through the exercise, using his model, of testing the effects of two separate stockpile transactions: a one-time 100,000 ton increase in the U.S. copper stockpile in 1960, and a sustained 100,000 ton annual increase in the stockpile beginning in 1960. These are both found to affect price only very slightly, by about 1 percent, and private stocks fall to compensate for the rise in public stocks.

Banks' book on the world copper market[31] does not contain a complete market model, though he discusses the appropriateness of several different modeling approaches. His supply-and-demand formulations make no mention of the U.S. stockpile.

Tinsley reviews four copper market models developed by private firms: those of Charles River Associates, Chase Econometrics, Commodities Research Unit, and Rio Tinto Zinc. He also discusses the published copper market model of Fisher, Cootner, and Baily. All the models reviewed involve varying degrees of complexity and simultaneity between national production in various countries, consumption, inventories, production capacity, scrap markets, substitutes, and prices. Tinsley does not mention the U.S. stockpile as a factor in any of these models.

LEAD AND ZINC

Gauntt regresses stockpile inventory on the difference between the lead or zinc price in year t and the average price over the four preceding years, using a simple one-equation model and data for the years 1950 to 1977. He finds strong evidence that the U.S. stockpile acted as an economic buffer stock for lead and zinc, with "a strong relationship between current market conditions and changes in government inventories."[32]

TIN

Baldwin's study of the world tin market[33] summarizes and discusses various tin models, noting that there have been only a few attempts to estimate demand-and-supply elasticities in the tin market. This is for good reason, he states:

The introduction of considerations such as uncertainty, risk aversion, cash-flow needs, capital availability, expectations of future costs and prices, and the theoretical framework for optimal exploitation of a fixed resource over time (i.e., economics of the individual mine), make it obvious that the functional relationship determining the responsiveness of tin output to a change in its price is far more complex than can be captured in an econometric model of a manageable level of abstraction or than can be tested with existing data.[34]

Baldwin spends pages discussing the impact of the U.S. stockpile on the tin market, however, and he believes that the stockpile is a major determinant of tin prices.[35]

Tin is included in Gauntt's single-equation model regressing stockpile inventory changes on 1950–1977 metal price data; he finds "a significant relationship exists between tin prices and inventory changes.... These findings imply that market conditions have significantly influenced tin stockpile activities." [36]

CONCLUSIONS: MODELING THE ROLE OF THE STOCKPILE IN PRICE DETERMINATION

In the aggregate, thus, many existing metal market models have acknowledged that the U.S. stockpile is important in price determination, though there is little consensus in the various models on how or where within the model to represent its effects. This is at least partly because of the wide range of market structures which exists for various metals, but the lack of consistency in modeling techniques means it is virtually impossible, using the diverse metal-specific models in the literature, to make cross-metal comparisons of stockpile effects or to arrive at conclusions about the stockpile's aggregate influence on metal markets. Discussion of the model used in the Appendix B addresses this issue in more detail. Nonetheless, the metal-specific models literature generally confirms that, where the stockpile has been tested as a price determinant, it has been found to be an important factor.

NOTES

1. See U.S. Congress, Senate, Armed Services Committee, Subcommittee on Military Construction and Stockpiles. *Hearings: Consideration of Stockpile Legislation.* 95th Congress, 2nd session, March 8 and 9, 1978, 131.

2. Gordon W. Smith, "U.S. Commodity Policy and the Tin Agreement," in David B. H. Denoon, *The New International Economic Order: A U.S. Response* (London: Macmillan, 1980), 18.

3. U.S. Congress, Senate, Armed Services Committee, Subcommittee on Military Construction and Stockpiles. *Hearings: Consideration of Stockpile Legislation.* 95th Congress, 2nd session, March 8 and 9, 1978, 90–92.

4. Examples of such government-to-government deals for stockpile transactions include the purchase of copper from Mobutu's Zaire in return for U.S. economic assistance in the mid-1960s, the sale of diamonds to the Israeli State Diamond Company in the early 1970s as part of the negotiations surrounding the Camp David Middle East peace accord, and the purchase of bauxite for the stockpile after Edward Seaga's election to Jamaica's presidency in the late 1970s.

5. U.S. Congress, Joint Committee on Banking. *Hearings: Defense Industrial Base. Part 3: New Stockpile Objectives.* 94th Congress, 2nd session, November 24, 1976, 67.

6. Ibid., 80.

7. Baldwin, 147.

8. United Nations, *Price Forecasting Techniques and Their Applications to Minerals and Metals in the Global Economy,* 3.

9. U.S. Congress, Senate, Armed Services Committee, Subcommittee on Military Construction and Stockpiles. *Hearing: Stockpile Commodity Legislation.* 96th Congress, 1st session, July 10, 1979, 10–11.

10. U.S. Congress, Senate, Armed Services Committee, Subcommittee on Military Construction and Stockpiles. *Hearings: General Stockpile Policy.* 95th Congress, 1st session, September 9, 1977, 82.

11. Robert A. Cornell, "United States Stockpile Policy," 3–6.

12. Cornell, 12.

13. Cornell, 16.

14. Cornell, 27.

15. Anderson, 143.

16. Anderson, 143–44.

17. United Nations, 51–53; Wagenhals, "Econometric Models of Minerals Markets," 86.

18. Haglund, *The New Geopolitics of Minerals: Canada and International Resource Trade,* 246.

19. United Nations, *Price Forecasting Techniques and Their Application to Minerals and Metals in the Global Economy,* 28. Many private-sector models are cited by name in the notes to this report.

20. Bension Varon, Wolfgang Glushke, and Joseph Shaw, *Copper: The Next Fifteen Years,* study done for the United Nations Centre for Natural Resources, Energy, and Transport (Dordrecht, Holland: D. Reidel, 1979), 1110–11. A list of various sources includes Terence D. Agbeyegbe, "Interest Rates and Metal Price Movements"; Walter C. Labys, "Commodity Price Stabilization Models" and "Commodity Markets and Models: The Range of Experience"; F. Gerard Adams, "Modeling of the World Commodity Markets"; John E. Tilton, "Cyclical Instability: A Growing Threat to Metal Producers and Consumers"; Gerhard Wagenhals, "Econometric Models of Mineral Markets: Uses and Limitations"; United Nations, *Price Forecasting Techniques and Their Application to Minerals and Metals in the Global Economy;* Robert S. Pindyck, "Gains to Producers from the Cartelization of Exhaustible Resources"; Albert L. Nichols and R. J. Zeckhauser, "Stockpiling Strategies and Cartel Prices," and R. V. Ramani, *Application of Computer Methods in the Mineral Industry.*

21. Labys, *Market Structure,* 4; Laursen and Yndgaard, 24.

22. Extensive bibliographies of these market-specific models are included in: Walter C. Labys, *Quantitative Models of Commodity Markets* (Cambridge: Ballinger, 1975); Gerhard Wagenhals, *The World Copper Market: Structure and Econometric Model* (Berlin/New York: Springer Verlag, 1984), 77–86; Gerhard Wagenhals, *A Bibliography of Econometric Non-Ferrous Metal Market Models* (Alfred Weber-Institut, University of Heidelberg, August 1983), and F. Gerard Adams and J. R. Behrman, *Econometric Modeling of World Commodity Policy* (Lexington, MA: Lexington Books, 1978).

23. Johnson and Rausser, 722; Labys, "Commodity Price Stabilization Models," 132. It would be interesting to investigate whether the U.S. stockpile has acted like a buffer stock to stabilize markets, using a model of the type discussed in Labys, "Commodity Price Stabilization Models," 128–30. This follows on the work of Gauntt. See also C. P. Brown, *Primary Commodity Control*, 140.

24. Ibid.

25. Douglas W. Woods and James C. Burrows, *The World Aluminum-Bauxite Market* (New York: Praeger, 1980).

26. Ibid., II-13.

27. Burrows, *Cobalt: An Industry Analysis.*

28. Ibid., 155–76.

29. UNCTAD, *Exploitation of the Mineral Resources of the Sea-Bed.*

30. Wagenhals, *The World Copper Market.*

31. Ferdinand E. Banks, *The World Copper Market: An Economic Analysis* (Cambridge: Ballinger, 1974).

32. Gerald E. Gauntt, "Market Stabilization and the Strategic Stockpile," 204.

33. William L. Baldwin, *The World Tin Market: Political Pricing and Economic Competition* (Durham, NC: Duke University Press, 1983).

34. Ibid., 110.

35. Ibid., 4–7, 55–87, 226–36.

36. Gauntt, 204.

Part III

The Stockpile and Metal Markets: Case Studies

Previous chapters indicate that the stockpile decision-making process actually was much more complicated than the Strategic and Critical Materials Stock Piling Act of 1946 specifically envisioned. How did all the relevant considerations interact in practice, and how did stockpile transactions actually affect metals markets? Specific examples in the case of several metals are discussed in the following five chapters.

7

Aluminum/Bauxite

Stockpile acquisitions and disposals of aluminum over the postwar period show a similar pattern to most other metals: massive purchases during the 1950s, which expanded world capacity well above normal market requirements, followed by reductions in the stockpile goals and sales of much of the metal over the 1960s and 1970s. Because of obligatory "buy-back" arrangements with the government, the same aluminum firms that originally supplied metal for the stockpile were forced to repurchase it when stockpile goals were reduced—thus inhibiting the industry's otherwise normal expansion. (Similar "buy-back" arrangements were instituted for other metals as well—for example, lead and zinc.)

Complained one mining industry representative in 1976, "The government's complete about-face in regard to stockpile requirements for aluminum played a significant role in the unsatisfactory price/cost relationships that have prevented the aluminum industry from earning a fair return on invested capital during much of the last 25 years."[1]

Threats of sales from the aluminum stockpile were used in 1965 to persuade domestic producers to withdraw a price increase which the government regarded as inflationary. When the small U.S. aluminum producer Olin Mathieson announced its intention of raising its domestic selling price for primary and fabricated aluminum, in late October 1965, other companies followed suit. The Johnson administration quickly announced that 200,000 tons of "surplus" aluminum would be released from the stockpile the following year. (The reasons cited were the steadily increasing demand stimulated by military production for the Vietnam War effort, and the balance of payments problems caused by meeting this demand through imports.) When the aluminum producers stood firm in their plans to raise prices, the government raised the quantity to be released by the GSA to 300,000 tons and announced the metal would be sold immediately. This persuaded the producers to withdraw their price increase and agree to the above-mentioned "buy-back" arrangement with the government.[2]

Nearly all the aluminum in the stockpile had been disposed of by the early 1970s. Nonetheless, a 1975 government study analyzed the possibility of using U.S. stocks as a weapon against the International Bauxite Association, in the aftermath of tax increases on bauxite exports by Jamaica and other producing nations. The study concluded that the total private and government-controlled aluminum inventories were only one-fourth to one-fifth the optimal size for them to be used in opposing a cartelization attempt by the IBA. "The most that could be hoped for is a credible threat [sic] to prevent the cartels from charging full monopoly prices. Staged sales ... may be required to make the stockpile a more potent weapon,"[3] stated a Congressional summary of the study's results. Not long afterward, the stockpile goals for aluminum were greatly increased.[4]

In late 1981, the GSA bought 25,400 tons of Chinese refractor-grade bauxite. An additional 75,000 tons of Chinese bauxite were purchased in 1984.[5]

In May 1982, by order of a presidential directive, a purchase/barter acquisition of Jamaican bauxite was initiated in conjunction with the administration's new Caribbean Basin Initiative. The bauxite was supplied from mines operated by Reynolds and Kaiser. Payment was half in cash and half in surplus U.S. agricultural products.[6] Jamaica also signed a contract with the U.S.S.R. in 1983, to sell one million tons of bauxite annually in return for machinery and other merchandise.[7]

States Anderson, "The political nature of (the U.S. bauxite purchase from Jamaica) is worth noting since bauxite was not considered a high-priority commodity for the stockpile."[8]

NOTES

1. U.S. Congress, Joint Committee on Banking. *Hearings: Defense Industries Base, Part 3: New Stockpile Objectives.* 94th Congress, 2nd session, November 24, 1976, 70.

2. Martin S. Brown and J. Butler, *The Production, Marketing and Consumption of Copper and Aluminum* (New York: Praeger): 156–57.

3. U.S. Congress, *Assessment of Alternative Stockpiling Policies.* Report prepared for the House Science and Technology Committee, 94th Congress, 2nd session, August 1976, 271.

4. U.S. Congress, House of Representatives, Armed Services Committee, Subcommittee on Seapower and Strategic and Critical Materials. *Hearings on H.R. 4895 a Bill to Amend the Strategic and Critical Materials Stock Piling Act.* 95th Congress, 1st session, March 14, 1977, 13.

5. U.S. Bureau of Mines, *Minerals Yearbook,* 1984, 141.

6. U.S. Bureau of Mines, *Minerals Yearbook,* 1981, 132, and 1983, 131.

7. U.S. Bureau of Mines, *Minerals Yearbook,* 1983, 139–40.

8. Anderson, 62 and 191.

8

Chromium/Manganese

The domestic chromite industry, which was virtually extinct in 1950 (there was only one producing mine in the United States),[1] received a new lease on life as a result of stockpile purchases in the early 1950s. By 1956, "at the close of four and a half years of development, nearly 3,000 people were directly or indirectly employed in chrome mining. Development costs and installed mill capacity [sic] were in excess of $5 million. Ore bodies in sight or reserves developed were capable of expanding rapidly to three or four times 1955 production," according to an industry spokesman's 1956 Congressional testimony.[2]

He also pointed out, in urging further stockpile purchases, that "mining is primarily done on Federal lands... It is not the type of industry to be turned on and off at will, therefore if not maintained, neglect very soon wastes completely the resources which might have been available in time of stress."[3]

Later in the same hearing, the U.S. Commodity Credit Corporation's barter program was discussed. This was a program designed to trade surplus U.S. agricultural products for less perishable foreign-produced commodities, mainly metals. Some of the metals obtained in this way went into the strategic stockpile; others were surplus to official strategic stockpile objectives and were simply stored by the agriculture department. Chromite was obtained from Turkey, Rhodesia, and South Africa in 1960–1961 through this barter program.[4]

The following interchange, between Senator Frank A. Barrett of Wyoming and T. R. Rawlings of the Department of Agriculture, concerning a trade of surplus U.S. wool for Turkish chrome, illustrates the sorts of considerations that played a part in these deliberations.

BARRETT: Mr. Rawlings, do you know what negotiations were made with Turkey sometime back with reference to the disposition of the wool stockpile, or some part of it, for strategic materials?

RAWLINGS: Yes, sir; we worked on that transaction for a number of months. Since our policy is to trade only through private United States firms, the firm that made the offer of the Turkish chrome for the wool was unable to furnish what we considered satisfactory financial guarantees, the same as we had required for the four-hundred-odd million dollars of materials that we had acquired up to that time [sic].

BARRETT: Did you have some assurance on that transaction that the Turkish Government would stand back of the transaction?

RAWLINGS: There were some assurances, sir, but on the other hand, we felt that if we were going to deal directly with the Turkish Government—and, incidentally, all of our barter transactions are through the private trade and not through the Government—then we would not have needed at all to have dealt with a private firm.

BARRETT: It strikes me that you are placing some undue restrictions on your activities in that regard that the Congress never imposed upon you and you are making it more difficult to get rid of these surplus stocks than you are required to do.

I think we would accomplish more from the Government standpoint if we get rid of these surpluses. If you fellows are going to sit over there and not make any effort to get rid of them and say, "We have to get gold for this stuff," we will never get rid of them....

Just keeping that stockpile of ... 120 million pounds of wool ... has cost the government $25 million the last year. So, in the first place, the wool was a threat over the market and it depressed the prices of the growers by about 100 percent in my judgement.

I believe if we had the blooming stockpile out of the way that the growers would get a better price and the requirements on the Treasury would be decreased at least by $25 million. That is my guess about the matter. That is why we have to find some way to loosen up this deal and accomplish two objectives: No. 1, get rid of all of the surplus stocks that we want to get rid of, and No. 2, get the best deal we can get for them in exchange.[5]

When asked about the market disruption effects of the barter program, Mr. Rawlings said,

We accept offer(s), timing the market right, in order not to raise prices. We take into account the domestic utilization of, say, chrome ore ... so that we don't go out and barter for more that will increase the price tremendously to domestic users here.... We do this in conjunction with our friends in the Emergency Procurement Service advising us, "Now, there is so much here you can possibly take without raising the price of this chrome." If we see the price is on the upgrade and a lot has been taken by domestic industry, we will pull out and wait a while.[6]

By 1956, the stockpile contained more than 100 percent of the defense stockpile objective and about 70 percent of the "long-term" objective for chromite. The GSA was paying $115 per ton for domestic chromite ore, while the world price for a comparable grade of ore was about $43 per ton.

Even the director of the U.S. Office of Defense Mobilization questioned, in Congressional testimony, whether this purchase program "would ultimately provide us with a mobilization base that would justify the expenditure of sums of money considerably in excess of the amounts that would be paid if the material were purchased on the world market."[7]

The advisability of government incentives for marginal mine development within the United States was revisited in 1984 in connection with a proposed cobalt project in northern California called the Cal-Nickel project. In a switch from earlier debates on such matters, California's Republican Congressional representatives *opposed* the use of federal funds for this development because of its environmental implications. Stated Congresswoman Barbara Boxer, "Many are concerned that the project threatens California's famous redwoods and others are concerned about the impact on the Smith River." Added Congressman Jerry Patterson, "Many concerns about the environmental effects and cost-effectiveness of the project have been raised.... I am not convinced that the expenditure of subsidies for domestic production of cobalt is the best use of U.S. taxpayer money."[8]

Some of the domestically mined chromite produced under contract especially for the stockpile was stored near a mine at Nye, Montana. The mine closed down when the GSA contract ended in 1961. After stockpile objectives were lowered in the early 1960s, the GSA attempted to sell this ore. However, there were no takers when it was offered on a competitive bid basis (FOB at Nye, Montana) from 1965 to 1968; the chromite was of low quality, and moreover, there was no railroad to the minehead, so transportation of the ore would have been a major problem.[9]

Chromite was one of the metals affected when "concentration factoring" was abolished in 1970. The objective for metallurgical grade chromite dropped from 3.65 million short dry tons (SDT) to 3.10 million, and the stockpile then held a surplus of 1.314 SDT. Other forms of chromium ore and metal were also in surplus at this point.

Government and industry representatives met in Washington on February 16, 1971 "to discuss the government's plan for additional disposal legislation and the development of a disposal plan. While the views of producers and consumers differ(ed) somewhat on disposal and proposed methods of sale, both the consumers and producers expressed a willingness to support the legislation," according to Congressional testimony of the Office of Emergency Preparedness' chief of the Stockpile Division, William N. Lawrence. The plan being considered was a long-term buy-back arrangement like that used for disposal of surplus aluminum, lead, and zinc.

A GSA official, in testimony about the same government-industry meeting, stated, "Industry expressed some concern [about the proposed chromium sale] in view of adverse market conditions prevailing in the chromium metal trade. We assured the industry that the excess chromium would be made available for disposal over a period of years with quantities and timing of disposals to be determined in the light of market conditions. Although the industry was not unanimous in its approval of the proposed legislation, we believe that if the legislation is approved, long-term agreements can be worked out whereby the industry will, over a period of years, work the Government excess material into their inventories and normal consumption pattern."[10]

Mr. L. G. Bliss, the chairman and CEO of a large U.S. chromium-using company, commented on the relationship between this stockpile release and the Rhodesia blockade:

There is nothing new about our industry's reliance on Federal stockpiles for a substantial portion of its requirements since 1966—the year before the sanctions against Rhodesia went into effect. Since 1968, our industry has received or contracted for some 982,000 SDT of chrome ore from Government stockpiles—or approximately 22 percent of the pre-sanction stockpile of 4,437,000 odd short dry tons.

The loss of Rhodesian ore to U.S. producers has had considerable impact upon our industry, and I might add, the steel industry as well....

Rhodesia formerly contributed about 40 percent of this Nation's requirement for metallurgical grade chromium ore. Despite increased shipments from the Soviet Union, Turkey and other producers, we have been unable to fill the vacuum created by the Rhodesian sanctions. Nor is there any realistic prospect for anything but a continued shortfall.[11]

He went on to point out that stockpile releases of chrome ore

might serve the temporary expedient of holding world chrome ore prices in line if not actually depressing them. The relief, however, can only be expected to be short-lived, since we are presently consuming chrome ore at a rate of over 800,000 SDT per year and could easily absorb the proposed offering in 14 to 15 months assuming no commitments to other suppliers. During this time, of course, far less foreign ore would be imported into the United States and our national inventory position would rapidly worsen.

With only 1.5 million tons of ore left in the stockpile, it is difficult to believe that we would again lower the objective and authorize an additional release. At that point, American producers looking to world sources for supplies would no doubt find that prices had climbed to their previous levels and perhaps beyond. And, of course, our national stockpile insurance would then be gone.[12]

This official's main point was thus to urge that chrome ore be exempted from the Rhodesian embargo. When questioned on whether he was opposed to stockpile chrome releases if an embargo exemption for chrome were not passed, Bliss said that was correct:

We feel that it is an imprudent act to sell off the one thing that has had some control over the climb in prices which, as I said, are now two and a half times presanction prices. If you trade that off I have no idea what those prices will become.[13]

This comment seems to indicate that at least one industry observer was aware of a potentially price-depressing role played by the stockpile chrome inventory, unrelated to actual sales from the stockpile.

In any case, sales of stockpiled chromite continued from 1964 through the early 1970s, during the years of the first Rhodesia boycott.

Just as for chromite, the domestic manganese purchase program authorized under the Defense Production Act resulted in the GSA's paying higher-than-market prices in the 1950s for U.S.-produced manganese ore and metal.

By 1956, the quantity of metallurgical manganese in inventory was more than the regular stockpile objective and amounted to about 90 percent of the "long-term" objective. In addition, large quantities of non-stockpile-grade ores had been bought under the domestic purchase program; it was unclear what specific processes could be used to beneficiate these low-grade ores or how much usable manganese could be obtained from them.

The U.S. government paid about $2.30 per long ton unit for the domestic specification-grade ore. At the time, the world market price for ore of the same grade was $1.30 per long ton unit.[14]

Manganese was sold from the stockpile through the early 1970s, on a negotiated contract basis. Stockpile sales stopped after 1976. In that year, the GSA established new stockpile goals for chromium and manganese, and also revised its stockpile purchase specifications. The Carter administration suspended the new stockpile goals when it took office in early 1977 pending further study, but reinstated the new goals later that year.

The Rhodesia embargo was reimposed in 1977 and finally removed in 1979. Prices for manganese and chromium were steady or falling by the late 1970s, owing to low consumer demand, heavy imports, and large private stocks. But in 1983, the GSA sold battery-grade manganese dioxide ore "to any party for consumption anywhere."[15]

Representatives of six manganese-producing nations (Brazil, Gabon, Mexico, Morocco, Upper Volta, and Zaire) met in September 1978 in Libreville, Gabon to discuss marketing and pricing problems in the industry, where the real ore price had shown constant decline since 1957, and to discuss a common position vis-à-vis consumers. The meeting, which was also attended by representatives of the United Nations Conference on Trade and Development (UNCTAD) and the United Nations Development Program (UNDP), proposed forming a "manganese forum" associated with UNCTAD, aimed eventually at an international commodity agreement between manganese producers and consumers.

In 1981, the U.S. manganese and chromium industries petitioned the federal government for "relief" under section 232 of the Trade Expansion Act of 1962. As a result, the U.S. Commerce Department investigated the effects of chromium ferroalloy and metal imports on national security; the National Security Council and the Office of Management and Budget also had input into recommendations which were made to the President in 1982.

This led to two U.S. government actions designed to assist the domestic ferroalloy industry: the reduction of preferential tariffs on chrome and manganese under the Generalized System of Preferences system, and a ten-year program of hiring U.S. producers to upgrade stockpiled chromium and manganese ores to metal. The President determined, however, that ferroalloy imports did not threaten to impair U.S. national security.

Beginning in 1983, contracts for the ore-to-metal stockpile upgrades were awarded to two U.S. firms (Macalloy Inc. and Elkem Metals Co.). Elkem was paid $9.8 million in 1984 to upgrade 48,000 tons of manganese ore to high-carbon ferromanganese; the company received $17.8 million in 1985, and $56 million in 1988 for similar work. Macalloy was paid $22.5 million in 1985 to convert 137,015 tons of chromium ore to 49,463 ton of ferrochrome for the stockpile.

Unlike the Rhodesia boycott situation, when sanctions were imposed on South Africa in 1986, both chromium and manganese were exempted by means of a certification by the Department of State that they were "critical strategic minerals unavailable from other sources," so imports from South African state-owned metals firms were allowed to continue.[16]

Sales of nonstockpile-grade manganese ore continued through the late 1980s, while prices declined. The motivations for these sales were various. In 1991, for example, the GSA sold ore stored in Butte, Montana which "needed to be removed to permit Superfund cleanup activities at that site."[17]

A comment by the U.S. Bureau of Mines in its 1991 *Minerals Yearbook* summarizes the political nature of the stockpiling program for manganese (and other ferroalloys):

The setting up and maintenance of a large stockpile has been the most tangible aspect of Government manganese programs. Management of the makeup, size, and disposition of this stockpile has been a key part of Government policy. Current law limits use of the stockpile to emergency situations, but its mere presence has had economic implications. Political developments during 1991 related to two foreign countries may lead to a reevaluation from the U.S. perspective of the strategic aspects of manganese, which could have a major impact on stockpile policy. The ending of U.S. sanctions against the Republic of South Africa diminished the possibility of a sanctions-related supply disruption. The lessening of international tensions accompanying transformation of the U.S.S.R. into a commonwealth of independent republics also seemed to favor lowered concern about potential deficiencies in the U.S.'s manganese supply.[18]

NOTES

1. U.S. Congress, Senate, Committee on Interior and Insular Affairs, Subcommittee on Minerals, Materials, and Fuels. *Hearings: Extension of Purchase Programs of Strategic and Critical Minerals*. 84th Congress, 2nd session, April 19, 20, 21, 25, May 16, 24, and 25, 1956, 46.

2. Ibid., 46–47.

3. Ibid.

4. U.S. Bureau of Mines, *Minerals Yearbook*, 1961, 435.

5. U.S. Congress, Senate, Committee on Interior and Insular Affairs, Subcommittee on Minerals, Materials, and Fuels. *Hearings: Extension of Purchase Programs of Strategic and Critical Minerals*. 84th Congress, 2nd session, April 19, 20, 21, 25, May 16, 24, and 25, 1956, 228–32.

6. Ibid., p. 232.

7. Ibid.

8. *Congressional Record*, 98th Congress, 2nd session, 1984, vol. 130, pt. 46; cited in Anderson, 82–83.

9. U.S. Bureau of Mines, *Minerals Yearbook*, 1958, 305; 1960, 341; 1961, 431; 1962, 412.

10. Ibid., 45.

11. Ibid., 47–48.

12. Ibid., 48.

13. Ibid., 53.

14. U.S. Congress, Senate, Committee on Interior and Insular Affairs, Subcommittee on Minerals, Materials, and Fuels. *Hearings: Extension of Purchase Programs of Strategic and Critical Minerals*. 84th Congress, 2nd session, April 19, 20, 21, 25, May 16, 24, and 25, 1956, 313.

15. U.S. Bureau of Mines, *Minerals Yearbook*, 1983, 594.

16. U.S. Bureau of Mines, *Minerals Yearbook*, 1991, 357 and 601–5.

17. U.S. Bureau of Mines, *Minerals Yearbook*, 1991, 968.

18. U.S. Bureau of Mines, *Minerals Yearbook*, 1991, 968.

9

Copper

The U.S. stockpile has exerted an important influence over the world market for copper. Stockpile sales of 250,000 tons in 1965–1967 were ordered by President Johnson expressly to slow price increases during the Vietnam War buildup. These came at a time when there was a copper strike in Chile, supplies from Zambia appeared to be in danger of being cut off due to civil unrest, and U.S. metalworkers' labor contracts were up for renewal. The stockpile sales apparently did hold prices down for a time, and possibly prevented price rises even larger than those that did occur later during the Vietnam War. However, the effect of the 1965–1967 sales, it has been asserted, was probably to delay the larger price increases rather than halt them altogether.[1]

GSA sales resumed in 1973—also for the expressed purpose of controlling prices. The 1973 sales, made by public auction during a period of price controls, saw stockpiled copper go for up to $1 a pound when the domestic producers' price was limited to 68 cents per pound—hardly an efficient exercise in inflation control. In any case, the question of whether this was an appropriate use of the stockpile did not receive much consideration.

U.S. foreign aid was used in conjunction with stockpile acquisitions to stimulate metals production abroad. For example, the U.S. provided a loan of 5 million pounds to the Rhodesian Selection Trust in 1951, which made possible the development of its Chibuluma copper and cobalt mine. Repayment of this loan, over ten years, was to be in metal (primarily cobalt) for the U.S. stockpile.[2]

There is evidence that copper stockpile goals have fluctuated with the availability of the metal on a barter-or-purchase basis from friendly countries such as Zambia. Commenting on a big increase in the copper stockpile goal in 1976 to more than six times the U.S. annual import requirement, S. D. Strauss of the American Mining Congress noted, "The increase ... should not be regarded as representing U.S. dependence on imports, but rather as a consequence of

Zambian desire for funds at a time when its normal European outlets are depressed." Others saw a possible desire to help Chile in the 1976 copper stockpile goal readjustment—though this was consistently denied by the administration, as in this exchange between Senator William Proxmire and General Leslie Bray of the Federal Preparedness Agency:

PROXMIRE: Well, take copper, for instance.

BRAY: Yes, sir.

Proxmire: Is the influence of the State Department with respect to Chile of any significance?

BRAY: No, sir.

PROXMIRE: Then why did we increase [objectives for] copper?

BRAY: Because our requirements exceed our production. It's as simple as that.

PROXMIRE: Well, if you could give us a detailed justification for the degree of increase there ...

BRAY: We would be glad to.[3]

A few years earlier, when the Chilean political situation was somewhat different, a memorandum from ITT urged the Nixon administration to delay purchases of copper from Chile in order to show disapproval of the socialist Allende government. Allende was deposed in a 1973 military coup supported by multinational copper firms.[4]

The stockpile sold 229,000 tons of copper in 1974. In 1976, a high new objective for copper was announced. However, no purchases ensued.

In 1985, according to the Bureau of Mines' *Minerals Yearbook*, "a group of U.S. Congressmen formed the Congressional Copper Caucus to lobby for the domestic copper industry. The 32 Senators and Representatives pursued legislation during the year to support the copper industry." Among the more than a dozen bills proposed were two relating to the strategic stockpile, and several aimed at limiting foreign copper production and imports. The copper goal remained much higher than the inventory at the time of transfer of responsibility for stockpile management to the Department of Defense in 1987.[5]

NOTES

1. U.S. Congress, House of Representatives, Armed Services Committee, Subcommittee on Seapower and Strategic and Critical Materials. *Hearings on H.R. 15081*. 94th Congress, 2nd session, August 26 and September 1, 1976, 6.

2. Cunningham, 104, 185, and 217.

3. Ibid., 32.

4. See Al Gedicks, *The New Resource Wars*, 1.

5. U.S. Bureau of Mines, *Minerals Yearbook*, 1987, 290.

10

Lead/Zinc

Like copper, lead and zinc have a domestic industry that has been able to muster considerable support via the stockpiling program.

In announcing the new "long-term" supplemental stockpile buying program in 1954 (which meant that lead and zinc were purchased despite the fact that the strategic stockpile objective for both metals had already been attained), President Eisenhower stated that this was preferable to imposing an import tariff on the metals, which he had also considered as a means of assisting the domestic lead/zinc industry. "It is my belief that the [supplemental stockpile purchases from domestic sources of up to 200,000 tons of lead and 300,000 tons of zinc] will help bring about the attainment of market prices for lead and zinc that are sufficient to maintain an adequate domestic mobilization base," Eisenhower declared. He promised "even more far-reaching measures" if the stockpile purchases were not successful in raising lead and zinc prices.[1] The *Wall Street Journal*, in a 1956 editorial, complained about the price-support aspect of the supplemental stockpile's operation during the Eisenhower administration.[2]

The question of fluctuating objectives for lead and zinc came up in a 1971 Congressional hearing on a stockpile disposals bill. William N. Lawrence, chief of the stockpile policy division of the Office of Emergency Preparedness, related how the objectives for lead and zinc were increased in 1969 from zero to 530,000 short tons and 560,000 short tons, respectively. He was questioned about this by Senator Howard W. Cannon of Nevada:

CANNON: How long was that objective zero for both lead and zinc?

LAWRENCE: It was zero from 1964 until 1969.

CANNON: That was a period of 5 years, why all of a sudden do we say we need to establish a requirement here?

Lawrence: Senator, this is not due to the commodity at all. It was due to the fact during that 4-year period we had a committee known as the Executive Stockpile Committee which was debating the stockpile policies as to how you determine objectives and it took them 4 years to come up with a policy and in that period very little was done on reviewing the objectives.

Cannon: That does not sound like a very good answer.

Lawrence: Well, it isn't a very good answer but unfortunately this committee membership, which was largely Cabinet level, was changed so that the policy kept getting reviewed over and over again.

Cannon: Are you satisfied now that the 530,000 tons of lead and 560,000 tons of zinc are adequate?

Lawrence: I certainly do [sic]. We have all of our requirements supplied through information on computers so we can run it without any great delay and we check on these things constantly.

Cannon: But you know in using a computer somebody has to be smart enough to put the information in the computer to start with.

Lawrence: I think we have some very good information in our stockpile computer now.[3]

In the same hearing, orderly disposal of remaining stockpile surpluses of lead and zinc was also discussed. A GSA official responsible for stockpile disposals, Mr. Bob Ross, related that the lead/zinc industry was increasingly reluctant to enter into long-term buy-back agreements due to "an apparent oversupply and high producer stock position, as well as other problems facing the industry."[4]

Such "buy-back" arrangements, Ross said, would work as follows:

The producers would undertake to purchase a fixed annual quantity which would dispose of the entire excess over a period of time with provision for a set-aside for nonparticipants. Each producer's share would be based on its production in certain years, to be adjusted periodically. However, the obligation to take deliveries was to be measured by the level of producer stocks on hand each calendar quarter. As a matter of fact, under this concept, with producer stocks of lead and zinc where they are now and have been for some time—the industry could not have taken delivery of one pound of material during such a period of high producer stocks on hand. However, with such an arrangement, ... it would be a simple matter [for the GSA] to respond to upward changes in the market [by releasing more lead and zinc].[5]

Clearly, the effect of these "buy-back" agreements would be to keep a lid on price increases in cases where large stockpile surpluses were available for release whenever supply tightened. But the GSA official nonetheless maintained, "The point we wish to emphasize again is that the disposal authorization we seek, be it in lead, zinc or any other material, does not warrant the concern of market disruption we frequently hear from representatives of industry. As stockpile managers, we seek the disposal authorization per instruction from the Office of Emergency Preparedness, with subsequent disposals as the particular industry can absorb the material."[6]

Lead and zinc industry representatives testified that they opposed the prospect of stockpile disposals; one corporate official stated,

I think the American industries' general feeling is we want to get rid of these stockpile surpluses, if you will, in the vernacular, we want them off our backs, and the lead-zinc industry feels similarly, but our own feeling is at this particular moment things are so bad that the very announcement in the press that a bill, even with the safeguard that Mr. Ross mentions, involving an additional half a million tons of lead and zinc which might come onto the market in the indeterminate future would be severely depressing. I guess what we are really asking is let's wait for a more appropriate time.[7]

NOTES

1. U.S. Congress, Senate, Select Committee on Small Business, Subcommittee No. 2. *Hearings: Problems Resulting from the Exclusion of Small Business from Stockpile Purchases and from Participation in the Disposal of Surplus Products Program.* 84th Congress, 2nd session, July 11, 12, and 17, 1956, 134.

2. Ibid., 135–36.

3. U.S. Congress, Senate, Committee on Armed Services, Subcommittee on National Stockpile and Naval Petroleum Reserves. *Hearing: Disposals from National and Supplemental Stockpiles.* 92nd Congress, 1st session, April 7, 1971, 56.

4. Ibid., 57.

5. Ibid., 58.

6. Ibid., 57.

7. Ibid., 63.

11

Tin

United States tin consumption has declined in the post–World War II period from about one-third of world tin production to less than one-fifth.[1] The strategic stockpile at one time held more than two years' worth of world production[2]—more than was ever in the international buffer stock of the International Tin Council.[3] For tin (like many other metals), post–World War II U.S. purchases for the stockpile kept world production in the late 1940s and 1950s at much higher levels than they would otherwise have been, thus stimulating overcapacity in relation to actual world consumption. This contributed to price stagnation once the large-scale U.S. purchases stopped in the 1950s. Some tin-producing interests did express unease at the implications of the United States' formation of such huge stocks, because of the bargaining power they gave the United States vis-à-vis the International Tin Council (which was formed in 1946 to represent both producers' and consumers' interests and help to stabilize prices). Provisions on the eventual liquidation of the stockpile were inserted in the International Tin Agreement. They limited the amount of tin the United States could release in any one year to 5,000 tons or 5 percent of the aggregate tin stockpile, whichever was less, and they required the United States to give the ITC at least three months' notice of any planned sales. (The United States did not join the ITC, and thus did not formally submit to such constraints on its stockpile disposals, until 1976—and then, only briefly.)

In 1955, there was about 350,000 tons of tin in the U.S. stockpile—an amount equivalent to seven years' worth of U.S. consumption and over two years' total world production. After 1962, the United States began disposing of this tin, bit by bit. Although disposals were generally discussed with the International Tin Council (which administered the International Tin Agreement and tin buffer stock for the purpose of stabilizing the world tin price), such consultations seldom involved ITC agreement that GSA tin sales were advisable.[4]

In the early 1960s, the GSA sold nearly 65,000 tons of tin at a time when the ITC buffer stock was depleted and world consumption was considerably outstripping production. At first, the tin price continued to rise despite the GSA sales. By 1965, however, tin prices began to fall, but GSA sales continued until mid-1968, despite ITC protests. The U.S. State Department also expressed concern to the GSA that these sales, while the ITC was *buying* tin to support the floor price, would have adverse political repercussions. In an informal agreement with the ITC in 1966, the GSA promised not to sell tin at times when the buffer stock manager was taking tin off the market.[5]

The tin sales during the 1960s were one result of the 1958 stockpile objective reductions from a five-year to a three-year supply. Even following a further objective reduction by President Nixon and the subsequent reinstatement of the three-year supply level by President Ford in the mid-1970s, the tin stockpile still held a large surplus—partly because of the continually declining use of tin in the U.S. economy, especially in food packaging. Large-scale GSA tin sales resumed in 1973 and 1974; again, world tin prices were rising due to the OPEC-generated commodities boom, and GSA sales did not contribute to absolute price declines, although they were equivalent to over 10 percent of world consumption in those two years. It is, of course, an open question how high the tin price would have risen in the 1960s and early 1970s without any stockpile sales.

When the United States joined the ITC in 1976, it agreed formally to consult with the ITC before selling tin from the stockpile to ensure that markets would not be disrupted, under the terms of the Fifth International Tin Agreement.[6]

The tin goal for the U.S. stockpile was reduced again in 1976, once more reflecting tin's declining use in food packaging and other industries.[7]

On December 21, 1979, after a long debate, Congress authorized the GSA to contribute 5,000 tons of stockpiled tin to the ITC buffer stock, and to sell 30,000 additional tons. The money earned from the tin sales was to be used to acquire other metals, particularly copper, for the stockpile. Members of Congress from copper-producing states lobbied hard for the inclusion of this provision. It was felt that the creation of a rotating stockpile fund (to be used for acquiring one metal from the proceeds of the sale of another) would minimize the possibility that budgetary considerations could enter into stockpile liquidation decisions— or as Representative E. H. Hillis of Indiana put it, that other governmental agencies would "raid the stockpile to sell off, or to put the dollars in the general Treasury ... for ... other things—with no sight at all on the strategic issues involved but as a way of raising some quick cash, so to speak."[8]

The Congressional debate also included lengthy consideration of the effect of the proposed GSA tin sales on world prices. Many witnesses before Congressional committees, and members of Congress themselves, expressed the view that the sales would lower tin prices, which would be beneficial for the U.S. economy. This was a major consideration in the decision to directly sell substantially more tin than was being contributed to the ITC buffer stock. Commented Representative William S. Moorhead of Pennsylvania, chairman of the House

Subcommittee on Economic Stabilization, which was considering the stockpile bill, "No one is making excessive claims for the anti-inflation payoff of this contribution [of tin to the ITC buffer stock]. Obviously more important is a separate proposal, not before this subcommittee, for the U.S. to sell unilaterally a much larger quantity of excess stockpile tin."[9]

The GSA in early 1980 announced its intention to auction off 10,000 tons of tin per year for three years—but it later postponed its initial sale until after July 1, 1980 at the request of the U.S. State Department, which was purportedly concerned about the sale's effect on the economy of Bolivia. Bolivia held its first democratic national election in thirteen years on June 29, 1980.[10]

Baldwin has described the effect of the GSA's ensuing tin sales in late 1980 and 1981, as the tin price first fell and then, with the entry of a "mystery buyer" of tin futures, rose to new heights. A combination of record-volume stockpile sales and changes in London Metals Exchange rules effectively squelched the market-cornering attempt of the "mystery buyer," who was eventually revealed to be an agent of the Malaysian government.[11] The effect of this incident was to demonstrate that the stockpile's managers would not hesitate to use it quite openly to oppose market trends they found objectionable.[12]

The "stabilizing" role of the U.S. stockpile has been emphasized by some studies of the world tin market. Even before the "mystery buyer" incident, various observers had noted that the U.S. tin stockpile seemed to defend an (unspecified, GSA-determined) price ceiling, while the ITC buffer stock generally defended the multilaterally determined floor.[13] This was at least partly because, in order to disrupt the market as little as possible, the GSA tried to sell its surpluses only when the price rose above some level that GSA considered to indicate world demand was outstripping supply. This price, whatever GSA decided it to be, became the effective world ceiling price, and GSA sales could thus counteract efforts by ITC members to raise prices through tin export control agreements, for example. In 1982, the U.S. stockpile was nearly four times as large as the ITC buffer stock.[14]

The GSA has insisted that its policy is not to sell in a period of falling prices (although, as noted above, this commitment to the ITC has been broken in the past), and that its rule of thumb is not to release more than 10 percent of U.S. annual consumption volume onto the market in any one year[15] (though this, too, has been contravened in years past). Nonetheless, the fact that, throughout the 1960s and 1970s, the GSA held huge amounts of tin that had been declared "surplus" and was thus ready to be sold whenever prices began to rise certainly appeared to be a powerful force keeping prices low. A further GSA contention, that the price at which stockpile sales were made did not differ substantially from the prevailing market price, was also disputed by producers. According to Noor Mohammed of the Malaysian Tin Bureau in Washington, quoted in 1983, "They have been disrupting the tin market both psychologically and physically.... In February 1983, they sold 485 tons, which isn't much, but it was priced two to three cents below the New York prices. The question is, who leads the price,

GSA or the (ITC) buffer stock manager?"[16] GSA official Carroll Jones retorted, "I'm not a price leader and I don't want to be.... If you look at the Reuter prices for the past month, you will see that we stay pretty much in step. We are not upsetting the tin market. If anyone is manipulating the market, it is not the U.S. government. We stabilize the market."[17]

Econometric models of the world tin market dating back to the mid-1960s have assumed that "sales out of consumer countries' stocks, especially the U.S. stockpile, assure that price does not go beyond the (ITC) ceiling price."[18] The Wharton Econometric model shows GSA sales as being about three times more important than ITC stocks in the years 1956–1973, with GSA defending the ceiling price through sales that were concentrated in periods of world shortage.

Of course, it is impossible to know by how much the tin price would have risen without the U.S. stockpile purchases which stimulated overcapacity before 1950, and the sales which dampened prices thereafter. The ITC view was that, although the precise impact of the U.S. stockpile was hard to determine, "there is no doubt that [if there had been no stockpile] production would have been larger over the last decade or so [1964–1974] and, in all probability, at higher price levels than we have in fact seen in that period."[19] Tin industry representatives and the Consumers' Union agreed, in making presentations before Congress, that stockpile sales helped to lower world prices,[20] and as detailed above, price stabilization and control certainly were important considerations in Congressional decision making concerning the tin stockpile.[21]

In 1983, because of continuing assertions by tin-producing countries that stockpile sales were harming their economies, the United States signed a memorandum of understanding with the Association of Southeast Asian Nations which limited GSA tin sales to 6,000 tons for 1983 and 1984.[22] The following year, GSA began a domestic tin disposal program, which involved "payments" of stockpiled tin materials to firms participating in upgrading stockpile ferroalloys. The bulk of GSA's tin disposals over the next four years were made under this swap program.[23]

Another effect of the stockpile seems to have been even more important than its overall lid on price increases, and that is its contribution to uncertainty. This has had many ramifications, such as a reduced propensity for U.S. tin-using firms to hold private stocks, once it was clear the stockpile supplies would be released in time of need,[24] reduced worldwide investment in tin mining and production,[25] and severe problems for the Bolivian tin industry, which was less able to weather price fluctuations since it operated at much higher costs and lower profit margins than the industries in the other three major tin-producing nations, Malaysia, Thailand, and Indonesia, (where the metal deposits are richer and closer to the surface of the ground).[26]

The delays inherent in the Congressional budget process were a major contributor to the uncertainty surrounding stockpile actions. For example, in 1976 and 1977, during a period of tin shortage, the GSA lacked Congressional authorization to sell stockpile surpluses. Permission was not received until mid-

1980, by which time production worldwide had reached a postwar high, but the sales proceeded nonetheless. Because Congressional actions are generally both slow and quite public, this may be the single most important focus of speculation in the world tin market. In a 1983 study of the market, William Baldwin noted:

No matter how careful and skillful GSA may be, and no matter how closely it may coordinate its disposals with the ITC, the overall political process by which the strategic stockpile policies have been formulated and changed has injected a major element of uncertainty and consequent price instability into the market. Recent market forecasts, based more on the predicted fortunes in Congress of one or more stockpile disposal bills than on estimates of production and demand, have often been inaccurate. Speculative price movements on the LME have responded sensitively to rumors and political events in Washington. Tin users have let stocks run down to very low levels in anticipation of disposal programs that failed to materialize and have then driven prices up in their efforts to restore normal working inventories. In an article written a year and a half before final passage of the 1979 Stockpile Act, the *Wall Street Journal* commented on one of the periods of greatest uncertainty, quoting a tin merchant as complaining, "Whenever Congress breathes, selling enters the market. It's ridiculous."[27]

For tin, one of the clearest examples of the stockpile's price effects occurred in 1963–1967. Large GSA sales followed a period of shortages on the world market, causing a long decline in prices from their peak in 1965. Says Baldwin,

It seems indisputable that the cause of the disturbance was the manner in which the U.S. stockpile loomed over the commercial market after announcement of the Congressional decision to reduce its size, and that the major stabilizing force was the market mechanism of producers' responses to price signals.[28]

The effect of U.S. stockpile sales may seem out of proportion to the volumes actually involved. In 1980, for example, the GSA was authorized to sell 10,000 tons of tin, or only about 5 percent of total world supply. But based on econometric estimates of world demand and supply elasticities, an increase in supply of 5 percent would lead to short-run price declines of 6 to 10 percent—hardly trivial. Moreover, the various uncertainties noted above apparently reinforced each other to heighten the impact of the U.S. stockpile. Noted the State of Malaya Chamber of Mines Year Book in 1980, "It is the threat to dispose of GSA tin and its ready availability rather than the actual disposals which disrupt the tin market. Although only 25 tons of GSA tin were sold in 1980, U.S. consumers know they can now purchase their requirements of tin on a day-to-day basis from the GSA if necessary. Plant inventories of tin have therefore been cut down to the bone."[29] According to the Wharton model, the major price effects of the U.S. stockpile can be directly attributed to such changes in the levels of private stocks.[30]

Proposals by the ITC and others that the United States adopt a clear, long-term policy of limiting its sales volume[31] or, better yet, that it contribute the tin deemed to be in "excess" to the ITC buffer stock[32] met with no response—or a negative one. Even the suggestion that the United States agree not to sell at prices below the ITC ceiling was not well received.[33]

Given the stockpile's long-term intensive involvement in the world tin market, it is clear that the stockpile is at least partly responsible for the ITC's eventual collapse. Market observers have attributed that collapse primarily to the insufficient resources that member countries were willing or able to devote to defending the tin price floor. Without the U.S. stockpile effectively defending the price ceiling over the previous twenty years, more resources would likely have accrued to the ITC since revenues from sales made at high prices would have gone to the ITC buffer stock instead of the U.S. government. This might have allowed the ITC buffer stock to defend the floor price more effectively and longer. The alternately ambivalent and hostile attitude of the United States toward the ITC is certainly consistent with the proposition that the stockpile had a role in hastening its demise.

The political questions raised by the U.S. government's use of the strategic stockpile are thorny ones, however. As for most industrial metals, governments have historically been closely involved in the workings of the tin industry, due to the existence of state mining corporations, as well as the ITC and the U.S. stockpile. As Baldwin notes, an unfortunate consequence of this governmental involvement is that "economic" conflicts can easily be escalated to the international political level. He points out, "The political repercussions of an aggressive cartelization attempt countered by an equally aggressive U.S. stockpile might be worse than the economic effects."[34]

NOTES

1. International Tin Council, *Conference on Tin Consumption* (London: ITC and Tin Research Institute, 1972), 23–24; also U.S. Congress, House of Representatives, Foreign Affairs Committee, Subcommittee on International Economic Policy and Trade. *Hearings: U.S. International Commodity Policy—Tin*. 95th Congress, 2nd session, February 15, 16, 21, March 1, and April 5, 1978, 13–14; and *Minerals Yearbook*, 1991, 1603.

2. William Fox, *Tin: The Working of a Commodity Agreement* (London: Mining Journal Books, 1974), 242.

3. Ibid., 109.

4. Ibid., 57–58. See also W. C. Labys, *Market Structure, Bargaining Power, and Resource Price Formation*, 127–28.

5. William Fox, *Tin: The Working of a Commodity Agreement* (London: Mining Journal Books, 1974), 348; William Robertson, *Tin: Its Production and Marketing* (London: Croom Helm, 1982), 147.

6. Baldwin, 59.

7. There were thirteen changes between 1944 and 1977 in the GSA's objective for the amount of tin to be reserved. (William Robertson, *Tin: Its Production and Marketing*, London: Croom Helm, 1982, 147).

8. U.S. Congress, House of Representatives, Armed Services Committee, *Full Committee Consideration of H.R. 4895*. 95th Congress, 1st session, March 17, 1977, 4.

9. U.S. Congress, House of Representatives, Banking, Finance and Urban Affairs Committee, 1. Other witnesses at Congressional stockpile hearings in the mid-1970s pointed out that in fact there would be little reason to believe stockpile sales would reduce long-run commodity prices; their price effects would generally be short-run only (U.S. Congress, House of Representatives, Armed Services Committee, Subcommittee on Seapower and Strategic and Critical Materials. *Hearings on H.R. 15081*. 94th Congress, 2nd session, August 26 and September 1, 1976, 5; Amos A. Jordan and R. A. Kilmarx, *Strategic Mineral Dependence: The Stockpile Dilemma* (Beverly Hills, CA: Sage Publications, 1979, 68). Speculators might benefit from the price swings, but the short-run lid on prices would tend to discourage investment in exploration and advanced production processes for the future (Jordan and Kilmarx, 68). Sales from the U.S. copper stockpile during the Johnson administration, and silver sales in 1973, which reduced short-run prices only to have them spring back to trend levels once the sales stopped, are examples. (Gordon W. Smith and G. R. Schink, "The International Tin Agreement: A Reassessment," *Economic Journal*, December 1976, 728; U.S. Congress, House of Representatives, Armed Services Committee, Subcommittee on Seapower and Strategic and Critical Materials. *Hearings on H.R. 15081*. 94th Congress, 2nd session, August 26 and September 1, 1976, 56–59.)

10. Baldwin, 59.

11. Ibid.; *Far Eastern Economic Review* (December 11, 1981): 81; *The Economist* (February 1983): 84; "Tin Producers and Buyers Battle on the International Market," *Multinational Monitor* (April 1982): 8; "Struggling Producers," *South*, May 1983, 72. Malaysian prime minister Datuk Seri Dr. Mahathir Mohamad, who came into office on July 15, 1981, was quoted the following month as saying, "If it is considered morally right for buyers to use stockpiles to lower prices, it is also morally right for sellers to use them to raise prices" (Baldwin, 5).

12. A GSA official stated at the time, "The buffer stock manager of the ITC thanked us for those sales because we helped prevent the Malaysians from cornering the market." ("Struggling Producers," *South*, May 1983, 72).

13. Baldwin, 61; Smith, "Commodity Instability and Market Failure," 2 and 13; Meghnad Desai, "An Econometric Model of the World Tin Economy, 1948–1961," *Econometrica*, January 1966, 109–10; also U.S. Congress, House of Representatives, Foreign Affairs Committee, Subcommittee on International Economic Policy and Trade, *Hearings: U.S. International Commodity Policy—Tin*. 95th Congress, 2nd session, February 15, 16, 21, March 1, and April 5, 1978, 39 and 48; and W. C. Labys, *Market Structure*, 128.

14. "Struggling Producers," *South* (May 1983): 72.

15. U.S. Congress, Senate, Armed Services Committee, Subcommittee on Military Construction and Stockpiles. *Hearings: General Stockpile Policy*. 95th Congress, 1st session, September 9, 1977, 82.

16. "Struggling Producers," *South* (May 1983): 72.

17. Ibid.

18. Desai, 109–10.

19. International Tin Council, *Fourth World Conference on Tin*, 69.

20. U.S. Congress, House of Representatives, Foreign Affairs Committee, Subcommittee on International Economic Policy and Trade. *Hearings: U.S. International Commodity Policy—Tin*. 95th Congress, 2nd session, February 15, 16, 21, March 1, and April 5, 1978, 83 and 114.

21. Jordan and Kilmarx, 67–68.

22. U.S. Bureau of Mines, *Minerals Yearbook*, 1983, 863.

23. U.S. Bureau of Mines, *Minerals Yearbook,* various years.

24. Baldwin, 61; Robertson, *Tin: Its Production and Marketing,* 148.

25. Robertson, *Tin: Its Production and Marketing,* 150.

26. Bolivia was the most vocal of the tin-producing nations in representing its case in Washington. The issue is a vital one for the Bolivian economy; as Representative Gilman of New York pointed out in one hearing: "The mere announcement of our intention to sell surplus tin stocks resulted in a severe price drop and a loss of revenue for Bolivia equal to nearly twice our current bilateral assistance program's level to that nation" (U.S. Congress, House of Representatives, Foreign Affairs Committee, Subcommittee on International Economic Policy and Trade. *Hearings: U.S. International Commodity Policy—Tin.* 95th Congress, 2nd session, February 15, 16, 21, March 1, and April 5, 1978, 225). Bolivia has consistently termed U.S. stockpile sales an "act of aggression against a friendly nation," and in 1979 it won a 13 to 12 vote of the Organization of American States condemning U.S. tin sales (Baldwin, 63). Bolivian representatives testified before Congress many times and lobbied hard to stop the sales (U.S. Congress, House of Representatives, Armed Services Committee. *Hearings: Full Committee Consideration of H.R. 9486 and Reprogramming Request No. FY 78-14.* 95th Congress, 2nd session, May 23, 1978, 7 and 11; also U.S. Congress, Senate, Armed Services Committee, Subcommittee on Military Construction and Stockpiles. *Hearing: Stockpile Commodity Legislation.* 96th Congress, 1st session, July 10, 1979, 13–40; U.S. Congress, House of Representatives, International Relations Committee, Subcommittee on International Economic Policy and Trade. *U.S. International Commodity Policies: Tin,* February 15, 16, 21, March 1, April 5, 1978, 44ff; also U.S. Congress, House of Representatives, Armed Services Committee, Subcommittee on Seapower and Strategic and Critical Materials. *Hearings on H.R. 9486, To Authorize a Contribution by the U.S. to the Tin Buffer Stock Established Under the Fifth International Tin Agreement.* 95th Congress, 2nd session, May 15, 1978, 34ff). Bolivia was supported by other tin-producing countries. One official of another tin-producing nation commented, "The Bolivians have been most outspoken, but you [the U.S.] had better take them seriously because they are speaking for a lot of others" (Baldwin, 100). Tin-producing countries had only a fraction of the access domestic interest groups have to the Congressional decision-making process, however. In stockpile hearings during the 1970s, U.S. industry representatives outnumbered those speaking for the producers' interests by at least 10 to 1.

27. Baldwin, 62–63.

28. Ibid., 137.

29. Ibid., 61.

30. Smith and Schink, 728.

31. Robertson, *Tin: Its Production and Marketing,* 149–50.

32. Smith, 19–20.

33. Ibid., 21.

34. Ibid., 236.

12

Conclusion:
The Stockpile's Market Influence

The institutional history and specific examples discussed in this book raise a number of points about the actual workings of the strategic stockpile. Clearly, "national defense" considerations are not sufficient to explain U.S. strategic stockpile policy. Other factors that have been involved in specific instances include balancing the government budget, reducing domestic inflation, limiting the bargaining power of commodity producers, foreign policy considerations, pressure from various domestic industry associations and other lobbying groups, desire to create or save jobs within the United States, and even what we may be called the "catch-all" factor: as the equipment and supplies arm of the U.S. government, the GSA is sometimes called upon to find a storage place, at no prejudice to the taxpayers, for supplies that are unneeded by other government agencies.

It is clear, in any case, that regarding the U.S. strategic stockpile as either simply "strategic" or purely "economic" would miss important aspects of its operations.

There is wide-ranging evidence from various metal industries that the stockpile is a major influence on market activity. Likewise, world price appears to be one of the factors that stockpile policy makers consider in deciding when and by how much to change stockpile inventories. This may be for any of several reasons:

1) the budget effects of commodity transactions are obviously dependent on world price;
2) world price trends are an indicator of whether stockpile sales (or purchases) are proving "disruptive" to world markets;
3) world price increases that seem to indicate market disruptions caused by other market actors (such as the Malaysian tin market-cornering attempt or the Rhodesian chrome boycott) have been seen as legitimate causes for intervention by the stockpile.

Thus, there are apparently mutual feedbacks between world price and stockpile policy.

Political considerations have also played a large role in stockpile decision making in specific cases. It seems difficult, however, to generalize about the exact form these political pressures have taken, which governmental actors were involved, or what sorts of domestic or foreign policy tradeoffs included the stockpile as a factor.

The stockpile's effects on metals prices seem to be due not only to its direct purchases and sales, but also to its effects on speculation and price instability (often via changes in the stockpile objective), the general profitability of mining and smelting industries (both domestic and foreign), producers' decisions with regard to expanding or reducing capacity, and the holding of inventories by private metal-consuming industries and by organizations such as the International Tin Council.

Congressional hearings and other documentary sources provide detailed evidence that decisions concerning the U.S. stockpile have often been made in an atmosphere of political posturing, where the original purpose and required procedures of the stockpile itself took a back seat to the more pressing considerations of budget, foreign policy, domestic economic stimulation, and political tradeoffs. This is partly due to the large degree of Congressional control mandated by early stockpile legislation, but it also results from subsequent legislation and presidential policies which have used the stockpile to accomplish other purposes, such as subsidizing U.S. metals producers or bartering away agricultural surpluses.

In each specific decision regarding stockpile policy—be it a relatively public, Congressionally debated one or the outcome of a confidential process within the GSA bureaucracy—one or more political factors may have been involved. Moreover, the outline of each debate and the particular factors that assumed relevance in each were usually not obvious, at least not until well after the issue was decided. Furthermore, throughout the stockpile's long existence, there has been considerable inconsistency in the outcome of these debates.

These historical and political issues become even more significant when viewed in the context of the stockpile's role as a major influence on world metals markets—markets which are vital to both metal-producing and metal-consuming countries. Given the complexity of these issues, it is appreciably easier to understand why studies of particular metal markets have treated the stockpile in both diverse and inconclusive ways. While acknowledging the stockpile's importance in price determination, most market modelers have nevertheless found themselves unable to accurately represent its effects—in particular, the demonstrated uncertainties of the political process attending the stockpile and the considerable likelihood of feedback effects between prices and stockpile actions.

This study shows that the stockpile, a factor common to many metal markets, has played significant role in influencing prices. By extension, because of this importance, the determinants of stockpile policy also become influential factors in metal markets. These determinants include U.S. import dependence, military expenditures, and especially political influences, which have a clear impact on U.S. policy determination.

In a broader sense, this study demonstrates some of the ways in which "micro" performance in individual markets is influenced by "macro" political-economy trends. The U.S. stockpile is a convenient focus for showing these influences, and it embodies many of the complexities that can be involved in the relationships between political and economic factors. These include the uncertainties and publicity of the political process which can contribute to speculation, the multilevel impacts of politically determined policies on markets (e.g., stockpile objective *and* inventory both proving important), and the wide variety of interrelationships that may be involved. For example, private inventories might be reduced in size because of the strategic stockpile's existence, stockpile policy might be used as a substitute for tariff policy to aid domestic metal producers; the stockpile may become a political pawn in a tit-for-tat settling of unrelated political or economic scores; and government transactions for the stockpile may take place at above- or below-market prices.

The importance of industrial metals in the U.S.—and the world—economy is increasing, not diminishing. Recent events in the former Soviet Union and Southern Africa, where major deposits of a number of strategic minerals are located, have led to considerable speculation and concern about fluctuations in these metals' availability on world markets. The U.S. strategic stockpile may thus be entering a period to which there will be renewed activity and interest in its existence. The kinds of effects described in this study will certainly continue to be felt in world metal markets for as long as a strategic stockpile remains.

Appendix A

Strategic and Critical Materials Stock Piling Act

SEC. 1. This Act may be cited as the "Strategic and Critical Materials Stock Piling Act."

FINDINGS AND PURPOSE

SEC. 2. (a) The Congress finds that the natural resources of the United States in certain strategic and critical materials are deficient or insufficiently developed to supply the military, industrial, and essential civilian needs of the United States for national defense.

(b) It is the purpose of this Act to provide for the acquisition and retention of stocks of certain strategic and critical materials and to encourage the conservation and development of sources of such materials within the United States and thereby to decrease and to preclude, when possible, a dangerous and costly dependence by the United States upon foreign sources for supplies of such materials in times of national emergency.

(c) In providing for the National Defense Stockpile under this Act, Congress establishes the following principles:

(1) The purpose of the National Defense Stockpile is to serve the interest of national defense only. The National Defense Stockpile is not to be used for economic or budgetary purposes.

(2) Before October 1, 1994, the quantities of materials to be stockpiled under this Act should be sufficient to sustain the United States for a period of not less than three years during a national emergency situation that would necessitate total mobilization of the economy of the United States for a sustained conventional global war of indefinite duration.

(3) On and after October 1, 1994, the quantities of materials stockpiled under this Act should be sufficient to meet the needs of the United States during

a period of a national emergency that would necessitate an expansion of the Armed Forces together with a significant mobilization of the economy of the United States under planning guidance issued by the Secretary of Defense.

MATERIALS TO BE ACQUIRED: PRESIDENTIAL AUTHORITY AND GUIDELINES

SEC. 3. (a) Subject to subsection (c), the President shall determine from time to time (1) which materials are strategic and critical materials for the purposes of this Act, and (2) the quality and quantity of each such material to be acquired for the purposes of this Act and the form in which each such material shall be acquired and stored. Such materials when acquired, together with the other materials described in section 4 of this Act, shall constitute and be collectively known as the National Defense Stockpile (hereinafter in this Act referred to as the "stockpile").

(b) The President shall make the determinations required to be made under subsection (a) on the basis of the principles stated in section 2(c).

(c)(1) The quantity of any material to be stockpiled under this Act, as in effect on September 30, 1987, may be changed only as provided in this subsection or as otherwise provided by law enacted after December 4, 1987.

(2) The President shall notify Congress in writing of any change proposed to be made in the quantity of any material to be stockpiled. The President may make the change effective on or after the 30th legislative day following the date of the notification. The President shall include a full explanation and justification for the proposed change with the notification. For purposes of this paragraph, a legislative day is a day on which both Houses of Congress are in session.

MATERIALS CONSTITUTING THE NATIONAL DEFENSE STOCKPILE

SEC. 4. (a) The stockpile consists of the following materials:

(1) Materials acquired under this Act and contained in the national stockpile on July 29, 1979.

(2) Materials acquired under this Act after July 29, 1979.

(3) Materials in the supplemental stockpile established by section 104(b) of the Agricultural Trade Development and Assistance Act of 1954 (as in effect from September 21, 1959, through December 31, 1966) on July 29, 1979.

(4) Materials acquired by the United States under the provisions of section 303 of the Defense Production Act of 1950 (50 U.S.C. App. 2093) and transferred to the stockpile by the President pursuant to subsection (f) of such section.

(5) Materials transferred to the United States under section 663 of the Foreign Assistance Act of 1961 (22 U.S.C. 2423) that have been determined to be strategic and critical materials for the purposes of this Act and that are allocated

by the President under subsection (b) of such section for stockpiling in the stockpile.

(6) Materials acquired by the Commodity Credit Corporation and transferred to the stockpile under section 4(h) of the Commodity Credit Corporation Charter Act (15 U.S.C. 714b(h)).

(7) Materials acquired by the Commodity Credit Corporation under paragraph (2) of section 103(a) of the Act entitled "An Act to provide for greater stability in agriculture; to augment the marketing and disposal of agricultural products; and for other purposes," approved August 28, 1954 (7 U.S.C. 1743(a)), and transferred to the stockpile under the third sentence of such section.

(8) Materials transferred to the stockpile by the President under paragraph (4) of section 103(a) of such Act of August 28, 1954.

(9) Materials transferred to the stockpile under subsection (b).

(b) Notwithstanding any other provision of law, any material that (1) is under the control of any department or agency of the United States, (2) is determined by the head of such department or agency to be excess to its needs and responsibilities, and (3) is required for the stockpile shall be transferred to the stockpile. Any such transfer shall be made without reimbursement to such department or agency, but all costs required to effect such transfer shall be paid or reimbursed from funds appropriated to carry out this Act.

AUTHORITY FOR STOCKPILE OPERATIONS

SEC. 5. (a)(1) Except for acquisitions made under the authority of paragraph (3) or (4) of section 6(a), no funds may be obligated or appropriated for acquisition of any material under this Act unless funds for such acquisition have been authorized by law. Funds appropriated for such acquisition (and for transportation and other incidental expenses related to such acquisition) shall remain available until expended, unless otherwise provided in appropriation Acts.

(2) If for any fiscal year the President proposes certain stockpile transactions in the annual materials plan submitted to Congress for that year under section 11(b) and after that plan is submitted the President proposes (or Congress requires) a significant change in any such transaction, or a significant transaction not included in such plan, no amount may be obligated or expended for such transaction during such year until the President has submitted a full statement of the proposed transaction to the appropriate committees of Congress and a period of 45 days has passed from the date of the receipt of such statement by such committees.

(b) Except for disposals made under the authority of paragraph (3), (4) or (5) of section 6(a) or under section 7(a), no disposal may be made from the stockpile unless such disposal, including the quantity of the material to be disposed of, has been specifically authorized by law.

(c) There is authorized to be appropriated such sums as may be necessary to provide for the transportation, processing, refining, storage, security, maintenance, rotation, and disposal of materials contained in or acquired for the stockpile. Funds appropriated for such purposes shall remain available to carry out the purposes for which appropriated for a period of two fiscal years, if so provided in appropriation Acts.

STOCKPILE MANAGEMENT

SEC. 6. (a) The President shall—

(1) acquire the materials determined under section 3(a) to be strategic and critical materials;

(2) provide for the proper storage, security, and maintenance of materials in the stockpile;

(3) provide for the upgrading, refining or processing of any material in the stockpile (notwithstanding any intermediate stockpile quantity established for such materials) when necessary to convert such material into a form more suitable for storage, subsequent disposition, and immediate use in a national emergency;

(4) provide for the rotation of any material in the stockpile when necessary to prevent deterioration or technological obsolescence of such material by replacement of such material with an equivalent quantity of substantially the same material or better material;

(5) subject to the notification required by subsection (d)(2), provide for the timely disposal of materials in the stockpile that (A) are excess to stockpile requirements, and (B) may cause a loss to the Government if allowed to deteriorate; and

(6) subject to the provisions of section 5(b), dispose of materials in the stockpile the disposal of which is specifically authorized by law.

(b) Except as provided in subsections (c) and (d), acquisition of strategic and critical materials under this Act shall be made in accordance with established Federal procurement practices, and, except as provided in subsections (c) and (d) and in section 7(a), disposal of materials from the stockpile shall be made by formal advertising or competitive negotiation procedures. To the maximum extent feasible—

(1) competitive procedures shall be used in the acquisition and disposal of such materials; and

(2) efforts shall be made in the acquisition and disposal of such materials to avoid undue disruption of the usual markets of producers, processors, and consumers of such materials and to protect the United States against avoidable loss.

(c)(1) The President shall encourage the use of barter in the acquisition under subsection (a)(1) of strategic and critical materials for, and the disposal under subsection (a)(5) or (a)(6) of materials from, the stockpile when acquisition or disposal by barter is authorized by law and is practical and in the best interest of the United States.

(2) Materials in the stockpile (the disposition of which is authorized by paragraph (3) to finance the upgrading, refining, or processing of a material in

the stockpile, or is otherwise authorized by law) shall be available for transfer at fair market value as payment for expenses (including transportation and other incidental expenses) of acquisition of materials, or of upgrading, refining, processing, or rotating materials, under this Act.

(3) Notwithstanding section 3(c) or any other provision of law, whenever the President provides under subsection (a)(3) for the upgrading, refining, or processing of a material in the stockpile to convert that material into a form more suitable for storage, subsequent disposition, and immediate use in a national emergency, the President may barter a portion of the same material (or any other material in the stockpile that is authorized for disposal) to finance that upgrading, refining, or processing.

(4) To the extent otherwise authorized by law, property owned by the United States may be bartered for materials needed for the stockpile.

(d)(1) The President may waive the applicability of any provision of the first sentence of subsection (b) to any acquisition of material for, or disposal of material from, the stockpile. Whenever the President waives any such provision with respect to any such acquisition or disposal, or whenever the President determines that the application of paragraph (1) or (2) of such subsection to a particular acquisition or disposal is not feasible, the President shall notify the Committees on Armed Services of the Senate and House of Representatives in writing of the proposed acquisition or disposal at least thirty days before any obligation of the United States is incurred in connection with such acquisition or disposal and shall include in such notification the reasons for not complying with any provision of such subsection.

(2) Materials in the stockpile may be disposed of under subsection (a)(5) only if the Committees on Armed Services of the Senate and House of Representatives are notified in writing of the proposed disposal at least thirty days before any obligation of the United States is incurred in connection with such disposal.

(3) The President may acquire leasehold interests in property, for periods not in excess of twenty years, for storage, security, and maintenance of materials in the stockpile.

SPECIAL DISPOSAL AUTHORITY OF THE PRESIDENT

SEC. 7. (a) Materials in the stockpile may be released for use, sale, or other disposition—

(1) on the order of the President, at any time the President determines the release of such materials is required for purposes of the national defense; and

(2) in time of war declared by the Congress or during a national emergency, on the order of any officer or employee of the United States designated by the President to have authority to issue disposal orders under this subsection, if such officer or employee determines that the release of such materials is required for purposes of the national defense.

(b) Any order issued under subsection (a) shall be promptly reported by the President, or by the officer or employee issuing such order, in writing, to the Committees on Armed Services of the Senate and House of Representatives.

MATERIALS DEVELOPMENT AND RESEARCH

SEC. 8. (a)(1) The President shall make scientific, technologic, and economic investigations concerning the development, mining, preparation, treatment, and utilization of ores and other mineral substances that (A) are found in the United States, or in its territories or possessions, (B) are essential to the national defense, industrial, and essential civilian needs of the United States, and (C) are found in known domestic sources in inadequate quantities or grades.

(2) Such investigations shall be carried out in order to—

(A) determine and develop new domestic sources of supply of such ores and mineral substances;

(B) devise new methods for the treatment and utilization of lower grade reserves of such ores and mineral substances; and

(C) develop substitutes for such essential ores and mineral products.

(3) Investigations under paragraph (1) may be carried out on public lands and, with the consent of the owner, on privately owned lands for the purpose of exploring and determining the extent and quality of deposits of such minerals, the most suitable methods of mining and beneficiating such minerals, and the cost at which the minerals or metals may be produced.

(b) The President shall make scientific, technologic, and economic investigations of the feasibility of developing domestic sources of supplies of any agricultural material or for using agricultural commodities for the manufacture of any material determined pursuant to section 3(a) of this Act to be a strategic and critical material or substitutes therefore.

(c) The President shall make scientific, technologic, and economic investigations concerning the feasibility of—

(1) developing domestic sources of supply of materials (other than materials referred to in subsections (a) and (b)) determined pursuant to section 3(a) to be strategic and critical materials; and

(2) developing or using alternative methods for the refining or processing of a material in the stockpile so as to convert such material into a form more suitable for use during an emergency or for storage.

(d) The President shall encourage the conservation of domestic sources of any material determined pursuant to section 3(a) to be a strategic and critical material by making grants or awarding contracts for research regarding the development of:

(1) substitutes for such material; or

(2) more efficient methods of production or use of such material.

NATIONAL DEFENSE STOCKPILE TRANSACTION FUND

SEC. 9. (a) There is established in the Treasury of the United States a separate fund to be known as the National Defense Stockpile Transaction Fund (hereinafter in this section referred to as the "fund").

(b)(1) All moneys received from the sale of materials in the stockpile under paragraphs (5) and (6) of section 6(a) shall be covered into the fund.

(2) Subject to section 5(a)(1), moneys covered into the fund under paragraph (1) are hereby made available (subject to such limitations as may be provided in appropriations Acts) for the following purposes:

(A) The acquisition, maintenance, and disposal of strategic and critical materials under section 6(a).

(B) Transportation, storage, and other incidental expenses related to such acquisition, maintenance, and disposal.

(C) Development of current specifications of stockpile materials and the upgrading of existing stockpile materials to meet current specifications (including transportation, when economical, related to such upgrading).

(D) Testing and quality studies of stockpile materials.

(E) Studying future material and mobilization requirements for the stockpile.

(F) Activities authorized under section 15.

(G) Contracting under competitive procedures for materials development and research to—

(i) improve the quality and availability of materials stockpiled from time to time in the stockpile; and

(ii) develop new materials for the stockpile.

(H) Improvement or rehabilitation of facilities, structures, and infrastructure needed to maintain the integrity of stockpile materials.

(I) Disposal of hazardous materials that are stored in the stockpile and authorized for disposal by law.

(J) Pay of employees of the National Defense Stockpile program.

(K) Other expenses of the National Defense Stockpile program.

(3) Moneys in the fund shall remain available until expended.

(c) All moneys received from the sale of materials being rotated under the provisions of section 6(a)(4) or disposed of under section 7(a) shall be covered into the fund and shall be available only for the acquisition of replacement materials.

(d) If, during a fiscal year, the National Defense Stockpile Manager barters materials in the stockpile for the purpose of acquiring, upgrading, refining, or processing other materials (or for services directly related to that purpose), the contract value of the materials so bartered shall—

(1) be applied toward the total value of materials that are authorized to be disposed of from the stockpile during that fiscal year;

(2) be treated as an acquisition for purposes of satisfying any requirement imposed on the National Defense Stockpile Manager to enter into obligations during that fiscal year under subsection (b)(2); and

(3) not increase or decrease the balance in the fund.

ADVISORY COMMITTEES

SEC. 10. (a) The President may appoint advisory committees composed of individuals with expertise relating to materials in the stockpile or with expertise in stockpile management to advise the President with respect to the acquisition, transportation, processing, refining, storage, security, maintenance, rotation, and disposal of such materials under this Act.

(b) Each member of an advisory committee established under subsection (a) while serving on the business of the advisory committee away from such member's home or regular place of business shall be allowed travel expenses, including per diem in lieu of subsistence, as authorized by section 5703 of title 5, United States Code, for persons intermittently employed in the Government service.

(c)(1) The President shall appoint a Market Impact Committee composed of representatives from the Department of Agriculture, the Department of Commerce, the Department of Defense, the Department of Energy, the Department of the Interior, the Department of State, the Department of the Treasury, and the Federal Emergency Management Agency, and such other persons as the President considers appropriate. The representatives from the Department of Commerce and the Department of State shall be Cochairmen of the Committee.

(2) The Committee shall advise the National Defense Stockpile Manager on the projected domestic and foreign economic effects of all acquisitions and disposals of materials from the stockpile that are proposed to be included in the annual materials plan submitted to Congress under section 11(b), or in any revision of such plan, and shall submit to the manager the Committee's recommendations regarding those acquisitions and disposals.

(3) The annual materials plan or the revision of such plan, as the case may be, shall contain—

(A) the views of the Committee on the projected domestic and foreign economic effects of all acquisitions and disposals of materials from the stockpile;

(B) the recommendations submitted by the Committee under paragraph (2); and

(C) for each acquisition or disposal provided for in the plan or revision that is inconsistent with a recommendation of the Committee, a justification for the acquisition or disposal.

(4) In developing recommendations for the National Defense Stockpile Manager under paragraph (2), the Committee shall consult from time to time with representatives of producers, processors, and consumers of the types of materials stored in the stockpile.

REPORTS TO CONGRESS

SEC. 11. (a) Not later than January 15 of each year, the President shall submit to the Congress an annual written report detailing operations under this Act. Each such report shall include—

(1) information with respect to foreign and domestic purchases of materials during the preceding fiscal year;

(2) information with respect to the acquisition and disposal of materials under this Act by barter, as provided for in section 6(c) of this Act, during such fiscal year;

(3) information with respect to the activities by the Stockpile Manager to encourage the conservation, substitution, and development of strategic and critical materials within the United States;

(4) information with respect to the research and development activities conducted under sections 2 and 8;

(5) a statement and explanation of the financial status of the National Defense Stockpile Transaction Fund and the anticipated appropriations to be made to the fund, and obligations to be made from the fund, during the current fiscal year; and

(6) such other pertinent information on the administration of this Act as will enable the Congress to evaluate the effectiveness of the program provided for under this Act and to determine the need for additional legislation.

(b)(1) Not later than February 15 of each year, the President shall submit to the appropriate committees of the Congress a report containing an annual materials plan for the operation of the stockpile during the next fiscal year and the succeeding four fiscal years.

(2) Each such report shall include details of all planned expenditures from the National Defense Stockpile Transaction Fund during such period (including expenditures to be made from appropriations from the general fund of the Treasury) and of anticipated receipts from proposed disposals of stockpile materials during such period. Each such report shall also contain details regarding the materials development and research projects to be conducted under section 9(b)(2)(G) during the fiscal years covered by the report. With respect to each development and research project, the report shall specify the amount planned to be expended from the fund, the material intended to be developed, the potential military or defense industrial applications for that material, and the development and research methodologies to be used.

(3) Any proposed expenditure or disposal detailed in the annual materials plan for any such fiscal year, and any expenditure or disposal proposed in connection with any transaction submitted for such fiscal year to the appropriate committees of Congress pursuant to section 5(a)(2), that is not obligated or executed in that fiscal year may not be obligated or executed until such proposed expenditure or disposal is resubmitted in a subsequent annual materials plan or is resubmitted to the appropriate committees of Congress in accordance with section 5(a)(2), as appropriate.

DEFINITIONS

SEC. 12. For the purposes of this Act:

(1) The term "strategic and critical materials" means materials that (A) would be needed to supply the military, industrial, and essential civilian needs of the United States during a national emergency, and (B) are not found or produced in the United States in sufficient quantities to meet such need.

(2) the term "national emergency" means a general declaration of emergency with respect to the national defense made by the President or by the Congress.

IMPORTATION OF STRATEGIC AND CRITICAL MATERIALS

SEC. 13. The President may not prohibit or regulate the importation into the United States of any material determined to be strategic and critical pursuant to the provisions of this Act, if such material is the product of any foreign country or area not listed as a Communist-dominated country or area in general headnote 3(d) of the Harmonized Tariff Schedule of the United States (19 U.S.C. 1202), for so long as the importation into the United States of material of that kind which is the product of such Communist-dominated countries or areas is not prohibited by any provision of law.

BIENNIAL REPORT ON STOCKPILE REQUIREMENTS

SEC. 14. (a) Not later than January 15 of every other year, the Secretary of Defense shall submit to Congress a report on stockpile requirements. Each such report shall include—

(1) the Secretary's recommendations with respect to stockpile requirements; and

(2) the matters required under subsection (b).

(b) Each report under this section shall set forth the national emergency planning assumptions used in determining the stockpile requirements recommended by the Secretary. Before October 1, 1994, such assumptions shall be based upon the total mobilization of the economy of the United States for a sustained conventional global war for a period of not less than three years. On and after October 1, 1994, such assumptions shall be based on an assumed national emergency involving military conflict that necessitates an expansion of the Armed Forces together with a significant mobilization of the economy of the United States. Assumptions to be set forth include assumptions relating to each of the following:

(1) Length and intensity of the assumed emergency.

(2) The military force structure to be mobilized.

(3) Losses from enemy action.

(4) Military, industrial, and essential civilian requirements to support the national emergency.

(5) Budget authority necessary to meet the requirements of total mobilization for the military, industrial, and essential civilian sectors.

(6) The availability of supplies of strategic and critical materials from foreign sources, taking into consideration possible shipping losses.

(7) Domestic production of strategic and critical materials.

(8) Civilian austerity measures.

(c) The President shall submit with each report under this section a statement of the plans of the President for meeting the recommendations of the Secretary set forth in the report.

DEVELOPMENT OF DOMESTIC SOURCES

SEC. 15. (a) Subject to subsection (c) and to the extent the President determines such action is required for the national defense, the President shall encourage the development of domestic sources for materials determined pursuant to section 3(a) to be strategic and critical materials—

(1) by purchasing, or making a commitment to purchase, strategic and critical materials of domestic origin when such materials are needed for the stockpile; and

(2) by contracting with domestic facilities, or making a commitment to contract with domestic facilities, for the processing or refining of strategic and critical materials in the stockpile when processing or refining is necessary to convert such materials into a form more suitable for storage and subsequent disposition.

(b) A contract or commitment made under subsection (a) may not exceed five years from the date of the contract or commitment. Such purchases and commitments to purchase may be made for such quantities and on such terms and conditions, including advance payments, as the President considers to be necessary.

(c)(1) Descriptions of proposed transactions under subsection (a) shall be included in the appropriate annual materials plan submitted to Congress under section 11(b). Changes to any such transaction or the addition of a transaction not included in such plan, shall be made in the manner provided by section 5(a)(2).

(2) The authority of the President to enter into obligations under this section is effective for any fiscal year only to the extent that funds in the National Defense Stockpile Transaction Fund are adequate to meet such obligations. Payments required to be as a result of obligations incurred under this section shall be made from amounts in the fund.

(d) The authority of the President under subsection (a) includes the authority to pay—

(1) the expenses of transporting materials, and

(2) other incidental expenses related to carrying out such subsection.

(e) The President shall include in the reports required under section 11(a) information with respect to activities conducted under this section.

NATIONAL DEFENSE STOCKPILE MANAGER

SEC. 16. (a) The President shall designate a single Federal office to have responsibility for performing the functions of the President under this Act, other than under sections 7 and 13. The office designated shall be one to which appointment is made by the President, by and with the advice and consent of the Senate.

(b) The individual holding the office designated by the President under subsection (a) shall be known for purposes of functions under this Act as the "National Defense Stockpile Manager."

(c) The President may delegate functions of the President under this Act (other than under sections 7 and 13) only to the National Defense Stockpile Manager. Any such delegation made by the President shall remain in effect until specifically revoked by law or Executive order. The President may not delegate functions of the President under sections 7 and 13.

UNITED STATES CODE CITATIONS

Section 2	-	50 U.S.C. 98a	Section 9	-	50 U.S.C. 98h
Section 3	-	50 U.S.C. 98b	Section 10	-	50 U.S.C. 98h-1
Section 4	-	50 U.S.C. 98c	Section 11	-	50 U.S.C. 98h-2
Section 5	-	50 U.S.C. 98d	Section 12	-	50 U.S.C. 98h-3
Section 6	-	50 U.S.C. 98e	Section 13	-	50 U.S.C. 98h-4
Section 7	-	50 U.S.C. 98f	Section 14	-	50 U.S.C. 98h-5
Section 8	-	50 U.S.C. 98g	Section 15	-	50 U.S.C. 98h-6
			Section 16	-	50 U.S.C. 98h-7

Source: U.S. Department of Defense, *Strategic and Critical Materials Report to the Congress.* Fiscal Year 1995, pp. 15–21.

Appendix B

Summary of Structure of Several Metal Market Models

A. ALUMINUM/BAUXITE

1. Woods-Burrows model[1] (3 equations, 2 prices)

Consumption (or Demand) = f_1 (Transactions Price; Exogenous Variables affecting Demand for Aluminum)

List Price = f_2 (Long Run Average Cost of Producing Primary Aluminum; Total Capacity; Consumption; Exogenous Variables affecting List Price, including dummy for U.S. government market intervention, 1953–1957 and 1972–1973)

Transactions Price = f_3 (Consumption; Total Capacity; Exogenous Variables affecting Transactions Price)

Variables for U.S. stockpile purchases and for shipments for defense applications were tested but not found to be significant.

B. COBALT

1. Burrows[2] (2 equations, Zaire acts as pricesetter)

Net Demand for Zairean Cobalt = f_1 (Exogenous Variables)

Zaire's Production Costs = f_2 (Exogenous Variables)

Zaire maximizes total profits subject to its net demand and cost functions; this gives Zaire's offer curve, which, set equal to total demand, gives price. The best price equation estimated was the following:

Price = f_3 (Total U.S. Industrial Consumption of Cobalt; U.S. Government Stocks of Cobalt; U.S. Government Net Purchases of Cobalt; Dummy for Demand Shifts due to Technological Change)

2. UNCTAD/ADAMS[3] (3 EQUATIONS):

Zaire's Cobalt Production = World Cobalt Consumption - Cobalt Produced by Other Suppliers as Copper By-product

Price Set by Zaire = f_1 (Rest of World's Cobalt Production + U.S. Stock Changes, including stockpile World Consumption or Demand)

Demand = f_2 (Price)

C. COPPER

1. Wagenhals[4] (3 main equations; Cobb-Douglas production function and 2 demand equations)

Mine Production Capacity, or Supply = (Bundle of Variable Inputs)^a x (Mine Production Capacity)^b

Demand for Consumption = f_1 (Copper Price; Aluminum Price; Index for Copper Users' Output; Dummy for 1966 U.S. copper strike)

Demand for Storage = f_2 (Past Inventories; Expected Copper Price; Opportunity Costs of Storage, or Interest Rate; Output of Copper-Using Industries)

Hypothesizes that copper producers maximize their profits given their capacity restrictions. Model also includes equations for secondary copper supply, various copper prices, East-West copper trade and U.S. refined copper production. Estimations are by OLS.

2. Banks[5] (not a complete model; market does not always clear, as evidenced by extensive producer rationing)

Supply = f_1 (Lagged Supply; Lagged Price)

Demand = f_2 (Lagged Demand; Lagged Price)

3. Fisher, Cootner, and Baily[6] (4 equations)

Supply = f_1 (Current Price; Lagged Price)

Demand = f_2 (Current Price; Lagged Price; Industrial Activity)

Price = f_3 (Lagged Price; Change in Stocks/Demand)

Change in Stocks = Supply - Demand

Divides world market into U.S., where prices are administered by government and U.S. producers, and rest of world, where prices are determined by free market forces of Supply and Demand, at the London Metals Exchange. The two areas are linked via LME price, trade, etc. Different Supply and Demand equations are estimated for the major producing and consuming areas, using the distributed lag response of Supply and Demand to prices. Demand is not disaggregated to end-use categories, nor are resources, capacity, technological variables, or prices of coproducts included.

D. TIN

1. Desai[7] (4 equations)

Demand = f_1 (Activity)

Supply = f_2 (Lagged Supply)

Change in Stocks = Supply - Demand

Price = f_3 (Stocks/Lagged Price)

Price was found not significant in either Demand or Supply, so was excluded from both.

2. Chhabra, Grilli, and Pollak[8] (2 equations)

Supply = f_1 (Lagged Price/Index of Mining Costs; Dummy for International Tin Council export control periods)

Demand = f_2 (Exogenous Variables)

Encountered difficulty in estimating Demand due to large number of end uses, changing user technologies, changing prices of substitutes and complements, and changing consumer tastes.

3. Lim[9] (Supply equation only)

Supply = f_1 (Lagged Price)

E. ZINC

1. Gupta[10] (7 main equations)

Mine Production, or Supply = f_1 (Lagged Price of Zinc; Index of Factor Prices; Mine Capacity; Index of Technological Change; Price of Coproducts)

Consumption, or Demand = f_2 (Price of Zinc; Activity Variable; Price of Substitutes)

London or Free Market Price = f_3 (Stock Consumption Ratio; Lagged U.S. Government Inventories; Lagged Change in U.S. Government Stocks; Lagged Price)

U.S. Price = f_4 (Change in U.S. Producer Stocks in Relation to Consumption; London or Free Market Price; Capacity Utilization Ratio)

Changes in U.S. Producer Stocks = U.S. Mine Production + Recovery from New Scrap + Recovery from Old Scrap + Net Imports into U.S. - U.S. Consumption - Increase in U.S. Government Stocks

Change in Stocks in Rest of World = Mine Production in Rest of World + Recovery from Scrap in Rest of World + Net Imports from East Bloc - Consumption in Rest of World - Net Exports to U.S.

Import Demand of U.S. Consumers = f_5 (Intermarket Price Differential between London and U.S.; U.S. Activity Variable)

Model also includes 2 equations for secondary Supply, dividing it into new scrap and old scrap. In estimation, it was difficult to get a significant coefficient on price, and often price was wrongly signed.

NOTES

1. Woods, Douglas W. and James C. Burrows. *The World Aluminum-Bauxite Market*. New York: Praeger, 1980.

2. Burrows, James C. *Cobalt: An Industry Analysis*. Lexington, MA: Lexington Books, 1971.

3. UNCTAD. Trade and Development Board. *Exploitation of the Mineral Resources of the Sea-Bed Beyond National Jurisdiction: Issues of International Commodity Policy*. New York: UNCTAD, 1973. (TD/B/449/Add.1)

4. Wagenhals, G. *The World Copper Market: Structure and Econometric Model*. Berlin/New York: Springer Verlag, 1984.

5. Banks, Ferdinand E. *The World Copper Market: An Economic Analysis*. Cambridge: Ballinger, 1974.

6. Fisher, F. M., P. H. Cootner, and M. N. Baily. "An Economic Model of the World Copper Industry." *Bell Journal of Economics,* vol. 3, no. 2, Autumn 1972, pp. 568–609. Summarized in Satyadev Gupta, *The World Zinc Industry,* (Lexington, MA: Lexington Books, 1982), pp. 93–94.

7. Desai, Meghnad. "An Econometric Model of the World Tin Economy, 1948–1961." *Econometrica,* vol. 34, no. 1, January 1966, pp. 105–34. See William L. Baldwin, *The World Tin Market: Political Pricing and Economic Competition* (Durham, NC: Duke University Press, 1983), p. 104, and Gupta, p. 92.

8. Chhabra, J. E., J. E. Grilli, and P. Pollak. *The World Tin Economy: An Econometric Analysis*. World Bank Staff Commodity Paper No. 1. Washington: World Bank, 1978.

9. Described in Baldwin, p. 108.

10. Gupta, Satyadev. *The World Zinc Industry*. Lexington, MA: Lexington Books, 1982.

Appendix C

Modeling Stockpile Effects in Metal Markets

The metal market literature and anecdotes reviewed in chapters 5 through 11 indicate that the stockpile has been—at least at times—an important factor in metal price determination. The diversity of the evidence provides support for a broad approach to modeling stockpile effects in order to shed light on the extent to which similar stockpile influences are common to many metals' markets.

The discussion of foreign and domestic political influences on stockpile policy in chapter 5 is underpinned by a vast political science literature which supports the position that industry lobbies, transnational corporations, representatives of foreign interests, and personal relationships or political obligations among decision makers all may be important factors in stockpile policy making. This literature suggests, however, that different bureaucratic and governmental actors tend to respond to the same range of political factors, so that a model that includes proxies for these factors may avoid becoming caught up in the details of the political process surrounding each particular stockpile decision.

These ideas, in conjunction with the historical literature on the stockpile discussed in chapters 1 through 4, provide the foundation for the model of stockpile policy making and price determination which is set out below. Unlike the specific metal market models discussed in chapter 6, this model focuses primarily on the interrelationships between U.S. stockpile transactions and metals price determination.

As noted in chapter 6, a wide variety of modeling approaches exists in the literature, and it is the opinion of some authorities that a composite approach to modeling may be more effective than a unilateral approach. The model which follows is, in this spirit, advanced as a fairly novel approach to metal market modeling which might serve as an input to other composite modeling processes and thus "enrich the information content of individual forecast models."[1]

Since U.S. government decision making with regard to the stockpile involves much more than the traditional determinants of supply and demand, this model, which focuses on the interrelationships between stockpile transactions and metals prices, necessarily incorporates theoretical insights from both economics and political science.

MODELING THE STOCKPILE'S PRICE EFFECTS

The historical material discussed above indicates that the stockpile may affect price determination either directly via its sales and purchases (changes in inventories), which represent changes in quantity demanded or supplied on the world market, or via expectations regarding its future actions (changes in objectives)—or both. Therefore, this study's model includes equations for the determination of the strategic stockpile objective (O), the stockpile inventory (I), and inventory change or sales and purchases by the stockpile (CI). The world price (PN) equation, which closes the model, includes these stockpile variables in its supply-and-demand specifications, presenting them in reduced form. The four equations form a simultaneous system and provide a representation of the interrelationships between the stockpile objective/inventory decision process and price determination in the international market.

The model is estimated using data on eleven important industrial metals. The metals were chosen on the basis of their importance for manufacturing and industry, as given by their relative ranking with regard to the market value of U.S. consumption. Table 4.1 (chapter 4) gives a comparison of the 1947, 1971, and 1993 rankings of metals by current market value of U.S. consumption. The eleven metals included accounted for 64 percent of the total appropriations made for the U.S. strategic stockpile as of December 31, 1947, and 63 percent of the stockpile's total value as of August 31, 1992.

The model is estimated for the entire group of eleven metals considered together, and then separately for each of the different metals being examined. These results enable statistical comparisons among estimated parameters of the different metals to be made, thereby permitting identification of the similarities and differences in the functioning of their markets. Of primary interest throughout is the significance of the strategic stockpile in world price determination for the metals, both individually and as a group.

The following sections discuss in turn the specification of each of the model's four equations, along with the expected signs on the variables included.

STOCKPILE OBJECTIVE

The Federal Emergency Management Agency (FEMA's) own statement on how stockpile objectives are determined[2] is taken as the starting point for the specification of the stockpile objective (see chapter 2). To recap, that document mentions U.S. import dependence and estimates of military needs as major factors in setting the "unadjusted stockpile goal." The stockpile objective, denoted by O in the model, is therefore taken to be a function of U.S. aggregate economic activity, which embodies both the cycles and the trend in U.S. economic growth (and thus in domestic demand for metals); U.S. military expenditures (as a proxy for both the "defense preparedness" emphasis and for the likelihood that stockpiles would actually be needed for strategic purposes), and U.S. import dependence (that is, U.S. consumption minus U.S. production). These variables are denoted as follows:

$A1$ = U.S. aggregate economic activity[3]

$A9$ = U.S. military expenditures[4]

$A10$ = U.S. import dependence (U.S. consumption minus U.S. production)

Expectations regarding the sign of variable $A1$ in the O equation are theoretically a bit complex. Aggregate economic activity certainly affects FEMA's estimates of the demand for a given metal throughout the U.S. economy (which in turn affects import dependence), but FEMA's interest would seem to be in ignoring cyclical effects when setting the long term strategic stockpile objective. However, FEMA might also see a cyclical upswing as evidence that larger quantities of a given metal are required to meet U.S. demand, and thus increase the stockpile objective. In this case, variable $A1$ would be expected to have a positive sign. In sum, a clear expectation regarding the sign of variable $A1$ is elusive.

U.S. military expenditures, variable $A9$, would be expected to have a positive sign in the O equation if FEMA's statement on how the stockpile objective is set is accurate. Variable $A10$, U.S. import dependency, would also be expected to have a positive sign, since metals for which the U.S. is highly import-dependent would need to be heavily stocked in order to meet U.S. needs in the event of a cutoff from external supplies.

As noted in chapter 2, the preliminary "unadjusted stockpile goal" is subject to revision by various government agencies based on their perceptions of "special circumstances" that warrant a revision. Although the specifics of this final review are not detailed in FEMA's explanation, there is evidence that domestic political and foreign policy factors seem to play a large role, given the wide fluctuations in stockpile objectives over the postwar years—of magnitudes that can hardly be explained by shifts in U.S. consumption, import dependence, or even defense expenditure patterns (see chapters 2 and 3, and Figures 1.1 through 1.11, chapter 1). The model therefore includes several political factors suggested by the literature as likely to be important in the stockpile decision process.

There are three steps in approaching the problem of how to represent these political effects: 1) Who makes the decisions setting the stockpile objectives? 2) What do these actors consider important in terms of domestic politics? 3) How can these considerations and priority rankings be reasonably approximated for inclusion in this model?

The answer to the first question is relatively straightforward, as discussed in chapter 2. The stockpile objective (as well as the inventory) is set through a complex and variable decision process involving government agencies, the presidential administration, and Congress.

The answer to the second question, what domestic political factors these decision makers consider important, is not easy to specify or generalize. The approach taken here is to propose several possibilities, which hopefully range across the spectrum of factors that actually enter into the stockpile decision process, for both Congressional and executive-agency actors.[5]

To summarize and elaborate upon the discussion in previous chapters, these factors include the following:

1) Voter/constituent interest in and response to stockpile decisions, particularly:
    a) those with jobs in industries affected
    b) those especially concerned with U.S. military preparedness and the "defense" rationale for the stockpile's existence.

2) Industry wishes and lobbying on the part of metal mining and smelting companies affected by stockpile decisions.

3) Interests of domestic metal consuming industries, and decision makers' perceptions of the broad effects of stockpile decisions throughout the economy.

4) Desire within the government to ensure readiness for a cutoff of foreign metal supplies by favoring the maintenance of domestic productive capacity even if private industry does not see this as profitable.

5) Desire to control inflation and recognition that the stockpile can be useful for this purpose, even though the law forbids its use in this way.

6) General influence of the U.S. military lobby for maintaining a strong "defense" capability and thus a substantial stockpile.

7) "Principled behaviour"—honest effort on the part of legislators and bureaucrats to do what is required by law and what is best for the country, whatever they discern this to be.[6]

8) Domestic political tradeoffs that involve the stockpile only incidentally, as a bargaining chip with which some actors may use their influence in return for others' cooperation on some unrelated issue.[7]

A full and precise model of the political decision-making process would arguably necessitate ranking, clarifying, and measuring the above, and perhaps other, factors. Since quantitative estimates of most of the above factors are not readily available, and since the focus of this study is not the political process *per se,* variables are constructed using existing data to provide several measures of domestic political factors based on the above discussion.[8]

If one takes the view that the direct will of voters is the most important determinant of both elected and civil service government officials' actions, then the domestic political factor of interest might be how many voters are affected by stockpile transactions. A more institutional view of the decision-making process, and one weighting Congressional input more heavily, would emphasize the number of members of Congress whose constituents are directly affected by stockpile decisions because of the presence of mines and/or smelters. It is possible to combine the effects of these two approaches, in a sense, by including the following variable:

D1 = the total population of states that produced the metal each year

These overall population figures are rough proxies for the number of Representatives in Congress who are likely to be closely concerned with the metal's industry because of their constituencies. The population figures may also proxy the magnitude of each metal's importance to other political or bureaucratic actors in the stockpile decision-making process.

Variable D1 would be expected to have a positive sign in the O equation. Industry lobbies and workers would be expected to want the stockpile to purchase the metal they produce, so as to raise its price and therefore their wages and profits. They would also resist and oppose stockpile sales. To the extent that the political influence of the metal-producing industries transmits itself via this population variable through to the stockpile decision-making process, objectives would be expected to be higher relevant to the more important the industry is within the United States.

A refinement of the previous variable would involve weighting the political sway of legislators from metals-producing areas more heavily if they sat on Congressional committees that were closely involved in making decisions concerning the stock pile. This can be approximated by:

D2 = the number of individual Senators representing each metal's producing states who sat on the Senate Armed Services or Appropriations committees, the Special Committee to Investigate National Defense Program, or the Joint Committee on Defense Production, each year

This variable would be expected to have a positive coefficient in the O equation, for the same reasons cited for variable D1 above. To avoid duplicating the effect of the domestic political influences that variables D1 and D2 are intended to capture, it is reasonable on theoretical grounds to include one or the other, but not both, in the O equation.

Several of the other factors noted in the political science literature as potentially important in stockpile decision making are proxied by other, not explicitly political, variables which are discussed below. For example, the lobbying abilities of large firms/transnational corporations may be proxied by the index of market concentration (variable A7).

International political interests also seem to be important in the domestic decision-making process concerning the stockpile. Such foreign policy considerations are most likely to enter the stockpile agenda via State Department or Presidential influence, though they may of course also be deemed important by Congressional or bureaucratic actors. Based on the institutional considerations discussed in chapters 2 and 3, examples of the types of foreign policy factors that may affect the stockpile are:

1) Desire to assist the economies of countries that are viewed as "friends" of the United States by purchasing metals they produce, or conversely, not to harm them by selling such metals.

2) Desire to boycott metal-producing countries viewed as "foes," or to ignore or to harm their interests in making sales.

3) Stockpile acquisitions as part of a package of foreign assistance to developing countries or as barter commodities in exchange for surplus U.S. agricultural products.

4) Response to international crisis situations with an increased emphasis on military preparedness and maintenance of the stockpile.

5) Lobbying by U.S.-based transnational corporations for purchases of (or against sales of) foreign-produced metals they handle.

6) The perception that supplies are more "secure" for metals supplied by countries that are friendly to the United States than for other metals, and that therefore the stockpile of these metals does not need to be as large.

Including such "foreign policy" factors in an econometric model is not easy, owing to data limitations and theoretical considerations. For example, proxying the "friends or foes" question by using the amount of foreign aid that metals-producing countries received from the United States or the former U.S.S.R. seems a reasonable approach during the Cold War years, but data are not available and consistent over the entire post–World War II period because foreign aid was not sent in significant amounts to many metal-producing countries until the 1960s. Even trade data for the U.S.S.R. are not available before 1954.

The volume of bilateral trade with the United States was thus decided upon as the best (albeit imperfect) way of representing whether metal-producing countries were "friends" or "foes" of the U.S. The following variable is included:

$F1$ = the value in U.S. dollars of U.S. exports to countries that are significant producers of each metal, taken as a proportion of total U.S. exports for the year

U.S. exports were used to measure the bilateral trade with each country, rather than U.S. imports, in order to avoid possible autocorrelation problems with other variables that are partially based on the volume of metals imported for the stockpile.

Variable $F1$ should serve as a proxy in the present model's estimation for the extent to which the producing countries are politically and economically aligned with or against the United States, and thus for the degree of risk, perceived by U.S. decision makers, that foreign cutoff of the metal would entail. In this sense, the coefficient of F1 would be expected to have a negative sign in the O equation, since the more closely aligned the producing nations are with the United States, the smaller the stockpile would have to be to safeguard U.S. supplies. However, to the extent that stockpile acquisitions are used as a substitute for other forms of foreign assistance to foreign metal-producing countries that are "friends" of the United States, the stockpile objective would be expected to be positively related to variable F1. This caveat is related to that discussed below for variable F1 in the CI equation, and it makes a sign expectation for F1 in the O equation quite problematic.

There are other foreign policy considerations that may affect the stockpile. Lobbying by foreign governments or their agents may play a role in stockpile decision making, but data or proxies concerning this are unavailable. Transnational corporations could use domestic influence in the United States to lobby for stockpile purchases of metals whose foreign production they control; this effect would probably not be captured by the domestic political variables included in the previous section. To test for the importance of this effect, a measure of the degree of "transnationalization" of each metals industry should be included (although this may, in fact, vary quite little among the different metals). Unfortunately, data on the percentage of world production handled by U.S.-based firms, for each metal in each year, is not available for the entire period, insofar as could be determined. Thus, although it would be interesting to test other foreign policy variables, this desire was stymied by data limitations.

To sum up the foregoing, the equation that represents the determination of the U.S. strategic stockpile objective for each metal j (j = 1,11) in each year t (t = 1,24) is as follows:

$$O_t^j = f_j(A1_t^j,\ A3_t^j \text{ or } A9_t^j,\ A10_t^j,\ D1_t^j \text{ or } D2_t^j,\ F1_t^j)$$

where

O = stockpile objective

A1 = U.S. aggregate economic activity

A3 = index of wars underway

A9 = U.S. military expenditures

A10 = U.S. import dependency

D1 = average population of U.S. states that produced the metal

D2 = number of senators from states that produced the metal who sat on key stockpile committees

F1 = U.S. exports to countries that produced the metal

Since all the explanatory variables are exogenous, the above equation can be estimated by Ordinary Least Squares and is recursive to the rest of the model.

STOCKPILE INVENTORY AND ITS CHANGE

Once the initial inventory at the beginning of the period under examination is given, the actual stockpile inventory, I, in each subsequent year can be determined using the perpetual inventory identity:

$$I_t^j = I_{t-1}^j + CI_t^j$$

In this model, the change in stockpile inventory from one year to the next—or the amount of each metal bought or sold by the GSA for the stockpile in each year (which is positive in sign for purchases and negative for sales)—is denoted by CI. Inventory change is taken to be a function of the difference between the stockpile objective (O) and actual inventory (denoted I), since presumably the GSA does attempt to bring the inventory into line with the stockpile objective.

However, since there is much evidence (as discussed in chapter 2) that this has generally not been accomplished, at least in the short term, other variables are included as well in the Inventory Change equation.

The difference between O and I is called variable OI (objective minus inventory). Its sign would be expected to be positive in the Inventory Change equation, since the larger the gap between objective and inventory, the more metal the GSA would have to buy to fulfill the stockpile objective.

Also included as determinants of inventory change are the same domestic and foreign policy factors that enter into the Objective equation (variables D1 or D2, and F1), since the decisions about when and how much to buy or sell, as described in chapter 2, are clearly subject to the same types of political disputes as the stockpile objective-setting process—although their importance may vary in the two processes.

Variables D1 and D2 would be expected to have positive signs in the CI equation, for similar reasons to those given for the Objective equation: political influence within the United States would be expected to be wielded in the direction of stockpile purchases (and away from sales) of metals that are produced in the United States.

Predicting the sign of the coefficient for variable F1 in the CI equation is complex. If the inventory level is below the objective, from a military preparedness point of view, one would expect purchases to take place faster for metals produced by U.S. "foes" than for metals produced by "friends"—thus if OI > O, the coefficient for F1 would be expected to be negative. However, purchases for the stockpile would be likely to have at least a short-term upward influence on prices for the metals bought, and if these are the products of U.S. "foes," this demand/price effect might be deemed undesirable by stockpile decision makers. On the same rationale as that used above to explain why domestic industries would lobby for stockpile purchases because of the price effects, U.S. "friends" would use their greater political leverage in the United States to push for stockpile acquisitions of the metals they produce. In this scenario, variable F1 would be expected to have a positive coefficient in the CI equation.

If the inventory exceeds the objective, from a purely pragmatic point of view, one might expect that the metal would be sold whether or not its producers were "friends" of the United States, so that if OI < O, the coefficient of F1 would again be expected to be negative in the CI equation. But would the U.S. government's desire not to harm "friends" by dumping the metals they produce outweigh the pure strategic assessment that those metals are less vital to the stockpile than those produced by "foes"? If so, the coefficient of F1 would be positive.

To summarize, it is difficult to predict the signs of F1's coefficient. We can, however, observe that if some metals show a positive coefficient for F1 in the CI equation where OI < O, this could indicate that foreign policy considerations played a role in increasing stockpile purchases to help foreign "friends" and/or delaying stockpile sales so as not to damage the interests of "friendly" producer nations even though the stockpile was oversupplied.

The historical literature outlined in chapter 2 suggests that the GSA may have been more eager to buy (and more reluctant to sell) metals for which there was a domestic U.S. industry than metals that were mainly produced abroad. An inter-active dummy (variable INT1) is included in the Inventory Change equation to test this hypothesis—that is, whether purchases are more likely and sales less likely for domestically produced metals than for other metals, when there is a discrepancy between I (stockpile inventory) and O (stockpile objective). Variable INT1 takes the value of OI (in other words, it is larger the larger the shortfall of inventory below the stockpile objective) for U.S.-produced metals, and it is zero for metals not produced in the U.S. Its coefficient in the CI equation would be expected to be positive if the hypothesis concerning differential treatment by the U.S. government for domestic versus foreign-produced metals is correct.

World price (denoted PN) is also included in the model as a determinant of inventory change. World price is the main index for government decision-makers of how costly a stockpile purchase is likely to be, and likewise an indicator of how much government revenue will be realized from a given sale of stockpile material.

There is little evidence from the institutional literature on the stockpile that its managers operate under a clear budget constraint; nevertheless the hearings material cited above does indicate that Congressional appropriations discussions have sometimes centered on the budgetary implications of stockpile sales or purchases. World price also proxies the relationship between supply and demand in the world market, and it is thus an important variable in the GSA's decision process by which changes in stockpile inventory are determined. Although its influence via the budget process is probably related to that of the domestic political and foreign policy variables included in matrices D and F, world price for each metal represents important current information available to government decision makers whose inclusion in the inventory-change equation is warranted in its own right.

The coefficient on world price in the Inventory Change equation would be expected to be negative, because of the budget/appropriations constraint under which the GSA and Congress operate (if the price of one metal is increasing, it may seem sensible to use limited resources to buy another and perhaps even to increase government revenue by selling the metal which is increasing in value— in effect, using the strategic stockpile as if it were an "economic" stockpile). Moreover, the sometimes-overt pressure for stockpile sales specifically for the purpose of controlling short-term price increases and inflation would also lead one to expect a negative sign on world price.

The full equation for change in the stockpile's inventory is thus as follows:

$$CI_t^j = f_2(OI_j^t, D1_t^j \text{ or } D2_j^t, F1_t^j, PN1_t^j)$$

where

CI = change in stockpile inventory

OI = objective minus inventory

D1 = total population of states that produced the metal

D2 = number of senators from states that produced the metal who sat on key Congressional stockpile committees

F1 = U.S. exports to countries that produced the metal

PN = world price

with the t subscripts indicating the year and the j superscripts indicating the particular metal, as before.

PRICE DETERMINATION

Since the object of this study is to test the importance in world price determination of U.S. stockpile-related variables (such as the stockpile objective, inventory, inventory change, and the price at which stockpile transactions were made), these variables are all included in the world price equation. The historical literature reviewed above suggests that both the change in inventory (CI) and the level of inventory (I) have the potential of affecting world price—CI through the usual market mechanisms, by increasing or decreasing quantities available on the market and thus, *ceteris paribus,* lowering or raising price, and I via expectations, insofar as it represents a threat to sell suddenly if price should change in a way that is unacceptable to the U.S. government. As noted, there are historical precedents for such uses of the stockpile.

Change in the level of the stockpile objective, CO, may in a similar way signal the importance accorded the metal by the U.S. government, which could also be a proxy for how vital controlling its price or its availability is to the United States. More significantly, both CO and the difference between the objective and the inventory (OI) supply clues to other market actors about whether the government is likely to be buying or selling in the near future. For these reasons, the variables CO and OI are also included in the price equation.

The price at which GSA transactions were made in each year (GN) represents perhaps the most concrete of the stockpile's influences on world markets, since the U.S. government conducted transactions of such large relative size during the period in question. As mentioned above, the price at which the GSA bought or sold metals could be significantly different from the prevailing world price since the GSA sometimes negotiated deals with metals producers for the large quantities it purchased, and sometimes acted for political reasons to subsidize metals producers and consumers when making purchases and sales of stockpiled metals. The variable GN is thus included as a determinant of world price in this model.

The metal market literature discussed in chapter 3 mentions a number of non-stockpile-related variables that have been found to be important in price determination, in previous studies of specific metal markets. These variables include technological change (on either the demand side or the supply side or both), the effects of dual markets or government intervention that prevents markets from clearing, labor market factors (strikes) or other supply disruptions (political disturbances in producer nations, for example), private stocks and inventory changes, factor costs, coproduct prices, mineral reserves or mine capacity, recycling or scrap utilization, changing substitution possibilities and characteristics of the markets of substitutes and complements, and variables that attempt to capture the effects of several different mining or production technologies' being employed at the same time. This study does not emphasize such market-specific factors, for the following reasons:

1) A pooled estimation of the model, using data for eleven metals together, is employed to arrive at conclusions regarding the stockpile's importance for major industrial metals overall.

This pooling technique reduces the importance of any given metal's specific market characteristics, while highlighting the factors common to all the markets considered. Omission of variables that may be determinants of price in one or a few of the eleven markets, but are irrelevant in the others, is thus theoretically reasonable.

2) International aggregate economic activity (variable A2) is included in the world price equation as a proxy of cyclical market activity. This variable also generally proxies several of the other factors mentioned above, such as private inventory activity, market characteristics of coproducts, substitutes, complements, and factor costs.

3) A market concentration variable (A7), included for theoretical reasons as discussed below, may also proxy some specific market characteristics (such as mining and production technology and the level of private inventories).

4) The satisfactory statistical results of price estimations using this specification indicate that the level of precision which might be attained by including more metal-specific variables is unnecessary for a broad general understanding of the markets' common characteristics.

World price is thus modeled for the purposes of this study as being a function of stockpile-related variables, plus market concentration and international aggregate economic activity.

In order to sort out the *a priori* expectations regarding the world price effects of these variables, an examination of the expected effects of each on world supply and world demand is needed. The resulting supply and demand equations can be set equal to each other and solved for price, which appears in both equations since world price is assumed to affect both world supply and world demand. This gives sign expectations for those variables which appear in one or both of the equations.

Clearly such a supply-and-demand approach to price determination is less than ideal, given the oligopolistic nature of all of the metal markets involved. For this reason, an index of market concentration for each metal (variable A7) is included, as mentioned above, in the world price equation. Further justification for the use of the usual market-clearing approach is referred to in the review of the literature on metal-specific market models in chapter 6.

SUPPLY AND DEMAND

On the demand side, if the stockpile objective is greater than the inventory (i.e., if $O > I$), then the stockpile is likely to be purchasing metal in the near future, which would cause the quantity demanded on the world market to increase and the world price to rise, *ceteris paribus*.

The supply-side impact of the relationship between stockpile inventory and stockpile objective would occur when there is a surplus of metal in the stockpile, i.e., when $O < I$ or when OI is negative. This would mean that surplus stockpiled metal could (by law) be released onto the market at any time (usually subject to Congressional approval), and the expectation would be that the quantity supplied to the world market would therefore increase.

The variable OI, with a lag of one year to allow the expectations about stockpile actions to have their impact on the market, should therefore appear in both the supply and demand equations, with a positive sign on the demand side and with a negative sign on the supply side. The lag is limited to one year because information about stockpile objective and inventory changes is public and there is no reason to believe the expectations concerning stockpile actions would take longer than one year to have their market effects.

At a second level, because of the political influences on the stockpile, market actors may realize that if the United States has a producing industry for the metal in question, a stockpile surplus is much less likely to be released than if the United States does not produce the metal. Therefore, we might expect little or no effect on supply, even if OI is negative, for metals produced domestically. Conversely, if purchases are expected, in order to bring inventories into line with objectives, these (with their accompanying demand effect) might be expected to be prompter for U.S.-produced metals than for others. This is tested separately, by including the interactive variable INT1 in the world price equation. As discussed above, INT1 takes the value of OI for domestically produced metals, and the value zero for all others. Variable INT1 should appear on both the supply and the demand sides, with a positive sign in both cases (since negative values for INT1 would correspond to the supply-reducing case, and positive values for INT1 would be associated with the demand-raising situation).

Actual stockpile sales and purchases should also be included in the world supply-and-demand equations, insofar as the stockpile itself contributes to world supply when it sells metals and is a component of world demand when it makes purchases. Thus, change in inventory or CI should appear in the supply equation with a negative sign, and in the demand equation with a positive sign.

The stockpile objective level is a step function, and changes in its level are reasonably strong indicators of stockpile policy changes that are likely to lead to sales or purchases. Change in objective would thus serve as a signal of U.S. government intentions and would be expected to affect world price accordingly. If CO is positive, the objective has increased, and purchases would be expected to follow; CO should therefore appear in the demand equation with a positive sign. If CO is negative, the objective has decreased and one would expect sales to follow, so CO should also enter in on the supply side with a positive sign.

The level of the stockpile inventory would affect world price insofar as it represents a quantity that could "hang over" the market and reduce the impact of production fluctuations. The larger the stockpiled amount in relation to world production, the larger this potential effect—so it is actually stockpile inventory as a proportion of world production, or I divided by variable A4 (world production), which should be included. If the stockpile is perceived to be "hanging over" the market, i.e., threatening to release large amounts of metal if the price begins to rise, this would be transmitted via the supply side; thus the variable I/A4 should appear in the supply equation, with a positive sign. There would be no corresponding demand-side effect.

As noted above, the GSA price at which stockpile transactions are made (GN) seemingly influences world price outside of the supply-and-demand framework. Variable GN might also be expected to affect world price by heightening the effect of stockpile sales if the U.S. government price is lower than the prevailing world price at the time of the stockpile sales, and conversely by heightening the impact of stockpile purchases if the U.S. government price is above the prevailing world price at the time of the stockpile purchases. In other words, if $CI < 0$, the stockpile is selling, quantity supplied on the world market is increasing, and price would fall *ceteris paribus;* and if at the same time $GN < PN$, the price would fall even more. By the same token, if $CI > 0$, the stockpile is buying and contributing to world demand, price would rise, and if $GN > PN$, indicating that the stockpile is buying at above-market prices (which has in fact happened when the United States wished to assist domestic producers or a foreign metals-producing country, for example), the price effects of the stockpile purchases would be even greater. These price effects of the government-price variable GN are captured using two interactive dummy variables. The first (INT2) is designed to be positive under the circumstances of the first case described above, and it appears in the supply equation, while the second (INT3) is positive when CI > 0 and GN > PN, and it appears in the demand equation. Each is expected to have a positive sign.

International aggregate economic activity (variable A2) appears in both the supply and demand equations; its sign is expected to be positive since cyclical upswings would be associated with increases in both supply and demand, and vice versa.

The market concentration variable (A7) appears only on the supply side. According to traditional economic theory, it would be expected to have a negative sign since highly concentrated industries would be expected to restrict output in order to take advantage of monopoly profits. However, nearly the opposite situation has also been described in the metal-market literature: it may be in oligopolistic producers' long-term interest to keep prices low (as long as the firms are making a reasonable profit), in order to keep their customers from substituting away to other metals or to plastics and other materials which would erode the long-term demand for their product. In this case, the expected sign for variable A7 would be negative. Economic theory thus provides no crystal-clear predictions about the expected sign of the market-concentration variable.

To summarize the factors mentioned above, the demand and supply equations of the model are as follows:

$$Q_d = f_d(OI_{-1}, CI, CO, A2, A7, INT1, INT3, PN)$$

$$Q_s = f_s(OI_{-1}, CI, CO, I/A4, A2, A7, INT1, INT2, PN)$$

More specifically, assuming linearity:

$$Q_d = a_o + a_1OI_{-1} + a_2CI + a_3CO + a_4A2 + a_5INT1 + a_6INT3 - a_7PN$$

$$Q_s = b_o - b_1OI_{-1} - b_2CI + b_3CO + b_4(I/A4) + b_5A2 - b_6A7 + b_7INT1 + b_8INT2 + b_9PN$$

Setting demand and supply equal and solving for PN yields:

$$Q_s - Q_d = 0$$

$$b_9PN + a_7PN = -b_o + b_1OI_{-1} + b_2CI + b_3CO - b_4(I/A4) - b_5A2 + b_6A7 - b_7INT1 - b_8INT2 + a_o + a_1OI_{-1} + a_2CI + a_3CO + a_4A2 + a_5INT1 + a_6INT3$$

$$PN = (a_7 + b_9)^{-1}\{(a_o + [(a_1 + b_1)OI_{-1}] + [(a_2 + b_2)CI] + [(a_3 - b_3)CO] + (a_4 - b_5)A2 + b_6A7 - b_4(I/A4) + [(a_5 - b_7)INT1] + a_6INT3 - b_8INT2\}$$

Since a_6 and b_8 are assumed positive, we expect a positive sign in the PN equation for the variables OI_{-1} and CI. We expect a negative sign for the variables I/A4 and INT2. The signs on CO, A2, and INT1 depend on the relative magnitude of the coefficients in the demand and supply equations, and thus are indeterminate in this general formulation. Variable A7 is also indeterminate in sign, while variable INT3 is expected to be positive.

The price equation in this model, as outlined above, differs slightly from the demand equation normally found in econometric models in which changes in price are related to changes in quantity demanded or quantity supplied. This is because the change in the stockpile objective, change in inventory, inventory level, and difference between objective and inventory (CO, CI, I, and OI) are all included in the P equation. Inventory change (CI) corresponds in a sense to a change in quantity in the usual formulation, but inclusion of change in the stockpile objective (CO) and the level of the inventory (I), as well as their difference (OI), is an unusual feature of this model.

Two additional variables, whose effects on supply and demand *per se* are indeterminate, are also included in the world price equation as a means of testing two more hypotheses concerning world price effects. First, GSA price itself (variable GN) is included, because of the extensive evidence that it often differs from the prevailing market price and because this differential seems likely to have an impact on world price in a more direct fashion than would be captured by the dummy variables INT2 and INT3. Second, an interactive dummy variable (MCOMP) is included to test whether there are any peculiarities in world price effects resulting from the fact that bauxite is aluminum ore, and thus the two markets are vertically integrated.

In very general form, then, the world price equation in the model is specified as follows:

$$PN_t^j = f_1^j[(OI_{t-1}^j), \ CI_t^j, \ CO_t^j, \ A_t^j, \ I_t^j/A4_t^j, \ INT1_t^j, \ INT2_t^j, \ INT3_t^j, \ GO_t^j, \ MCOMP_t^j]$$

This equation is simultaneously determined with the CI equation, which includes PN as an argument.

THE COMPLETE MODEL

The complete model employed in this study can now be summarized as follows:

$$PN_t^j = f_1^j[(OI_{t-1}^j), \ CI_t^j, \ CO_t^j, \ A2_t^j, \ A7_t^j, \ I_t^j/A4_t^j, \ INT1_t^j, \ INT2_t^j, \ INT3_t^j, \ GN_t^j, \ MCOMP_t^j]$$

$$O_t^j = f_2^j(A1_t^j, \ A3_t^j \ or \ A9_t^j, \ A10_t^j, \ D1_t^j \ or \ D2_t^j, \ F1_t^j)$$

$$I_t^j = I_{t-1}^j + CI_t^j$$

$$CI_t^j = f_3^j(D1_t^j \text{ or } D2_t^j, F1_t^j, OI_t^j, PN_t^j)$$

where the j superscript indexes particular metals (j = 1,11) and the t subscript indexes years in the period 1947–1992 (t = 1, 44), and:

O = stockpile objective

CO = change in stockpile objective since previous period

I = stockpile inventory

CI = change in stockpile inventory since previous period

A3 = index of wars underway

A2 = international aggregate economic activity

A4 = world production

A7 = index of market concentration

A9 = U.S. military expenditures

D1 = total population of metal-producing states

D2 = senators from metal-producing states on key stockpile committees

F1 = U.S. export to metal-producing countries

PN = world price

GN = GSA price

INT1 = dummy variable for objective-inventory differentials of U.S.-produced metals

INT2 = dummy variable for stockpile sales at below-market prices

INT3 = dummy variable for stockpile purchases at above-market prices

MCOMP = dummy variable for interaction between the aluminum and bauxite markets

The model is recursive with the O equation estimated first by Ordinary Least Squares and the other two behavioral equations estimated subsequently using simultaneous equation techniques.

MODEL IMPLICATIONS

The model's four equations—which specify the determination of the three stockpile variables O, CI, and I, plus world price PN—summarize the major hypothesis to be tested in this study: namely, that the stockpile objective, sales and purchases for the stockpile, and the inventory at a given point in time are determined in a process that affects, and is affected by, the world price.

The model is first estimated using pooled data on all eleven metals being considered, which allows general conclusions to be made across all metals and over time. Pooling allows comprehensive hypotheses to be tested concerning the stockpile's importance, apart from the specific characteristics of individual markets. All stockpile variables are expressed as percentages of world production in the pooled estimation of the model.

Separate estimation of the model for each of the eleven metals examined then allows a comparative assessment of the importance of each of the variables for each metal. For example, does the GSA price tend to have an upward influence on the world price of metals that are produced within the U.S. in significant quantity, and a downward influence on the world price of metals that are largely produced abroad? The metal-by-metal estimations of the model make possible comparative conclusions.

MODEL ESTIMATION AND RESULTS

The four-equation model set out in the previous section was estimated, first by Ordinary Least Squares (OLSQ) and then by the simultaneous estimation technique of Two-Stage Least Squares (2SLS). Where necessary, corrections for first-order serial correlation were employed. Based on the results of these preliminary estimations, the model was modified to remove highly correlated variables and those which in general proved to be insignificant.[9]

After these modifications, the final model had the following specific form:

$$PN_t = f_1(OILAG_t, CI_t, CO_t, A2_t, A7_t, GN_t, INT2_t, INT3_t)$$

$$O_t = f_2(A1_t, A9_t, A10_t, D2_t)$$

$$I_t = I_{t-1} + CI_t$$

$$CI_t = f_3(D2_t, OI_t, PN_t)$$

This model was estimated over the forty-four-year period using data for all eleven metals. The estimation results are given in Table C.1.

RESULTS OF THE POOLED MODEL

As shown in Table C.1, the pooled estimation of the model yielded satisfactory results. Based on the adjusted R^2, the World Price equation "explained" 28 percent of the variation in world price over the period in the simultaneous estimation, and the Objective equation "explained" 18 percent of variation in the stockpile objective levels. The Inventory Change equation captured 20 percent of the variation in the change in inventories in the 2SLS estimation.

RESULTS OF THE WORLD PRICE EQUATION

With regard to this study's main intention—assessing the impact of stockpile variables on world price—the results of the pooled estimation were striking. For the eleven metals together, the GSA price was significant at the 10 percent confidence level in explaining changes in World Price, while the dummy variable

Table C.1
Results of Pooled Estimations of the Model

Variables	Expected	2SLS Corr.[a]
World Price Equation		
Constant		5.958
Objective—Inventory, lagged one year (OILAG)	+	-0.075
Change in Inventory (CI)	+	0.034
Change in Objective (CO)	+	-0.011
World Agg. Econ. Activity (A2)	+	0.017***
Market Concentration (A7)	+/-	-0.135
GSA Price (GN)	+	0.025*
Dummy for GSA Sales at Below-Market Prices (INT2)	+	1.744**
Dummy for GSA Purchases at Above-Market Prices (INT3)	+	0.256
Metal Dummies		
MALU		-7.277
MBAU		2.554
MCHR		-2.520
MCOB		63.165
MCOP		-9.456
MLEA		-12.388
MMAN		-0.107
MMOL		28.486
MNIC		14.205
MTIN		18.233
Durbin-Watson Statistic		1.30
Adjusted R^2		0.28
Rho		0.827***
Objective Equation		
Constant		0.46
U.S. Agg. Econ. Activity (A1)	+/-	-0.87
U.S. Military Expenditures (A9)	+	0.12
U.S. Import Dependence (A10)	+	-0.02***
Senators from Metal-Producing States on Key Committees (D2)		+0.05*
Metal Dummies		
MALU		2.89
MBAU		7.47*
MCHR		2.88

Table C.1: (continued)

Variables	Expected	2SLS Corr.[a]
MCOB		-0.44
MCOP		0.26
MLEA		-1.48
MMAN		3.12
MMOL		0.13
MNIC		-0.79
MTIN		-0.71
Durbin-Watson Statistic		1.89
Adjusted R^2		0.18
Rho		0.96***
Inventory Change Equation		
Constant		0.097
Senators from Metal-Producing States on Key Committees (D2)	+	-0.518
Objective—Inventory (OI)	+	-1.176***
World Price (PN)	-	-0.142
Metal Dummies		
MALU		-0.367
MBAU		0.014
MCHR		-0.096
MCOB		0.146
MCOP		0.197
MLEA		-0.034
MMAN		-0.066
MMOL		-0.195
MNIC		0.248
MTIN		-0.350
Durbin-Watson Statistic		2.07
Adjusted R^2		0.203
Rho		-0.347***

a. Results from estimations with a correction for autocorrelations.

* Coefficients are significant at the 10 percent confidence level (t-statistic > 1.282).

** Significant at the 5 percent confidence level (t-statistic > 1.645).

*** Significant at the 1 percent confidence level (t-statistic > 2.326).

designed to test for the price effects of GSA sales at below-market prices, INT2, also proved to be significant at the 5 percent confidence level.

The sign on the stockpile variable CI (Change in Inventory) was as expected: increasing purchases for the inventory were associated with increasing world prices. However, signs on lagged objective minus inventory (OILAG) and change in objective (CO) were opposite to what was expected. This indicates that falling prices are associated with increasing stockpile objectives and vice versa, while larger differences between stockpile objective and stockpile inventory in the previous year were associated with falling prices despite the implication that a large inventory-objective differential should lead the GSA to buy metal and thus influence the price upward. These results indicate that the stockpile's market effects are none too predictable or straightforward.

However, the statistical results indicate that the price at which the GSA buys or sells metal seems to be a significant influence on world metals prices, and that the stockpile variables taken together were indeed important predictors of world metal price trends.

Market concentration (A7) had the opposite sign in the estimated World Price equation from that normally predicted by monopoly theory. Instead of influencing prices upward, high market concentration in the model was associated with lower prices.

As discussed above, this may be because producers in highly concentrated industries had a long-term interest in keeping their customers from substituting away from their product, and thus could maximize their overall long-term profits by keeping prices relatively low.

Among the interactive dummy variables tested, both INT2 and INT3 proved significant in the 2SLS estimation. These variables were expected to have positive signs, because GSA purchases at above-market prices would be expected to influence world prices upward while GSA sales at below-market prices would be expected to influence prices downward. In the estimation, both hypotheses were borne out.

The metal-specific dummy variables had much larger estimated coefficients, in general, than the other variables. These dummy variables indicate the average differences in market characteristics and absolute price level between zinc and each of the remaining ten metals. In the World Price equation, their coefficients ranged from -0.117 for manganese to 63.165 for cobalt. This indicates that world prices were quite different with respect to which particular metal was being considered—which clearly makes sense insofar as some metals (e.g., manganese, nickel, tin) are much more valuable than others (e.g., bauxite, molybdenum) per short ton.[10]

RESULTS OF THE OBJECTIVE EQUATION

U.S. Import Dependence (A10) was significant at the 1 percent confidence level in the stockpile Objective equation, though it had the opposite sign from that which was expected. Instead of high import dependence being associated with high stockpile objectives, objectives were found to be lower for metals not produced in the United States. At the same time, the domestic political variable D2 (Senators from Metal-Producing States on Key Stockpile Committess in Congress) was significant at the 10 percent confidence level. This seems to indicate that domestic political factors were important determinants of stockpile objectives, and that objectives were kept high for metals produced within the United States.

The signs on the other variables in the Objective equation were consistent with expectations: U.S. military expenditures were positively associated with increased stockpile objectives, and U.S. aggregate economic activity was negatively associated with increased objectives, perhaps confirming that objectives are set countercyclically.

These results may be taken to indicate that FEMA's document which stresses the importance of domestic economic trends and U.S. import dependency in the stockpile objective-setting process was broadly accurate—although the FEMA document makes no mention of domestic political influences on the process, which were apparently also quite important. The extensive institutional literature which discusses the role of domestic political considerations in the stockpile objective-setting process is reinforced by this quantitative result.

Just as in the World Price equation, the individual metal dummies were very strong influences on variation in stockpile Objective. Once again, they reflect average differences in objective between zinc and the remaining metals. Their estimated coefficients ranged from -1.478 for lead to 7.474 for bauxite. This result is not surprising, since the average stockpile objective in short tons (which is a step function) was set by the GSA at different levels for different metals over the time period.

RESULTS OF THE INVENTORY CHANGE EQUATION

The difference between stockpile objective and inventory was found to be highly significant (at the 1 percent confidence level) in explaining changes in the stockpile inventory. However, this variable had the opposite sign from what was expected. Reinforcing the indication noted above that the differential between objective and inventory seems to have influenced prices downward, the results for inventory change indicate that large objective-inventory differences were associated with inventory changes which would increase those differences instead of reducing them.

Sign expectations were confirmed for world price in the inventory change equation (higher prices associated with fewer purchases, and vice versa). However, it was expected that more senators on important stockpile committees would lead to purchases for the stockpile, and this was not borne out by the statistical results.

In the Inventory Change equation, the metal-specific dummy variables (with estimated coefficients ranging from -0.066 for manganese to 0.248 for nickel) again show that the average magnitude of changes in stockpile inventory differed with each specific metal considered.

TESTS FOR CONTINUITY THROUGHOUT THE PERIOD

To test whether these results were consistent throughout the forty-four-year period, the pooled model was also estimated using data from just the first half of the period (1947–1971). This estimation would be expected to include more dramatic evidence of stockpile influences, because it covers the time during the 1950s when massive stockpile purchases of many metals were being made, and ends just before commodity prices fluctuated widely in the mid-1970s after the OPEC fuel price increase and the end of the gold standard. The results of this estimation are reported in Table C.2.

The general conclusions are as follows:

- Based on adjusted R^2s, the model "explains" changes in price, stockpile objective, and inventory change better for the first half of the period than for the entire forty-four-year span as a whole.
- In the price and objective equations, the signs on all statistically significant variables were as expected. In the inventory change equation, however, the variable OI (objective minus inventory) showed a negative sign, opposite to that expected, as discussed above, and this variable was significant at the 1 percent confidence level.

These results underscore the conclusion noted above for the period as a whole that GSA's purchase and sale decisions apparently are based on more than domestic political factors, world price, and the objective-inventory differential.

- Generally, there are no large discrepancies between results for the first half of the period and the period as a whole. The model predicts fairly well, just as for the period as a whole.

INDIVIDUAL METAL ESTIMATIONS

Full results of the model's estimation for each of the eleven individual metals are given in Tables C.3 through C.5.

The R^2's for most of the individual metal estimations of the model were quite low, which is not surprising given the special characteristics of each market and the generality of the model. The purpose of these individual estimations is not accuracy in depicting all activity in each metal's market so much as the possibility of comparing metals with regard to the importance of the U.S. stockpile.

When the results of the individual metal estimations are tallied (see Table C.6), the model is seen to have predicted fairly well, especially in the case of the World Price equation. Seven of the metals showed "correct" signs on lagged

Table C.2
Results of Pooled Estimation for Non-U.S.-Produced Metals, 1947–1971 Data Only

Variables	Expected	2SLS Corr.[a]
World Price Equation		
Constant		1.902
Objective—Inventory, lagged one year (OILAG)	+	0.111
Change in Inventory (CI)	+	0.141
Change in Objective (CO)	+	-0.264
World Agg. Econ. Activity (A2)	+	0.620
Market Concentration (A7)	+/-	-0.015
GSA Price (GN)	+	0.011***
Dummy for GSA Purchases at Above-Market Prices (INT3)		-0.189
Metal Dummies		
MALU		3.377
MBAU		-1.972
MCHR		-2.152
MCOB		43.979***
MCOP		5.677*
MLEA		-0.295
MMAN		-0.233
MMOL		29.881***
MNIC		18.252***
MTIN		27.997
Durbin-Watson Statistic		1.88
Adjusted R^2		0.58
Rho		0.854***
Objective Equation		
Constant		-0.390
U.S. Agg. Econ. Activity (A1)	+/-	-0.151*
U.S. Military Expenditures (A9)	+	-0.123
U.S. Import Dependence (A10)	+	0.361***
Senators from Metal-Producing States on Key Committees (D2)	+	0.095**
Metal Dummies		
MALU		1.050
MBAU		8.957
MCHR		4.812
MCOB		1.447
MCOP		1.388

Table C.2: (continued)

Variables	Expected	2SLS Corr.[a]
MLEA		0.054
MMAN		6.580
MMOL		0.935
MNIC		1.140
MTIN		1.333
Durbin-Watson Statistic		1.83
Adjusted R^2		0.54
Rho		0.69***
Inventory Change Equation		
Constant		0.242
Senators from Metal-Producing States on Key Committees (D2)	+	-0.016
Objective—Inventory (OI)	+	-1.326***
World Price (PN)	-	-0.011
Metal Dummies		
MALU		-0.721
MBAU		-0.048
MCHR		-0.177
MCOB		0.341
MCOP		0.383
MLEA		-0.063
MMAN		0.014
MMOL		-0.080
MNIC		0.483
MTIN		
Durbin-Watson Statistic		2.05
Adjusted R^2		0.41
Rho		-0.316***

a. Results from estimations with a correction for autocorrelation.

* Coefficients are significant at the 10 percent confidence level (t-statistic > 1.282).

** Significant at the 5 percent confidence level (t-statistic > 1.645).

*** Significant at the 1 percent confidence level (t-statistic > 2.326).

Table C.3
Individual Metal Results—World Price Equation

Metal Estimation Method	ALU OLS[a]	BAU 2SLS[a]	CHR 2SLS[a]	COB 2SLS[a]	COP 2SLS[a]	LEA 2SLS[a]	MAN 2SLS[a]	MOL 2SLS[a]	NIC 2SLS[a]	TIN 2SLS[a]	ZIN 2SLS[a]
Variables											
Constant	4.24***	0.31***	1.46***	-924.61**	16.37***	5.94***	4.29**	23.79	19.04*	-132.03**	3.02***
Objective—Inventory, lagged one year (OILAG)	0.03	-0.02*	-0.31	3848.83	3.50***	1.55**	0.14	-2.09	-0.73	4.86	0.64
Change in Inventory (CI)	0.18	0.04	0.17**	-1795.18	-3.42	-4.34**	0.02	-0.88	0.49	-0.38	-0.56
Change in Objective (CO)	-0.30	-0.79	0.02	2821.79	2.81***	1.09*	0.20	2.42	-0.28	2.84	-0.44
World Agg. Econ. Activity (A2)	0.72	-0.13***	0.24	0.26**	-0.63***	0.47	0.20	0.04**	0.71	0.04***	0.12
Market Concentration (A7)	0.37	0.24**	-0.02***	11.00**	-0.21***	-0.12*	-0.04*	-0.06	-0.04	2.24***	-0.84
GSA Price (GN)	0.12	0.16	0.01*	0.02	0.05***	-0.82	0.40	0.06	-0.04	0.06*	-0.19
Dummy for GSA purchases at above-market prices (INT3)	0.36	0.21	0.04**	2.19	-0.82*	0.21	0.04	-1.56	0.45	-5.73	-0.34*
Durbin-Watson statistic	1.88	2.18	1.89	1.51	1.87	1.85	1.38	1.12	1.64	1.80	1.38
Adjusted R²	-0.04	0.30	0.66	0.14	0.72	0.22	0.08	-0.03	-0.13	0.18	0.05
Rho	0.63***	0.79***	0.49***	0.61***	0.20*	0.70***	0.80***	0.69***	0.63***	0.91***	0.60***

a. Results from the 2SLS estimation with a correction for autocorrelation. (2SLS results were corrected for autocorrelation if their Durbin-Watson statistics fell outside the range between 1.78 and 2.22.)

* Coefficients are significant at the 10 percent confidence level (t-statistic > 1.318) for a one-tail test.

** Significant at the 5 percent confidence level (t-statistic > 1.711).

*** Significant at the 1 percent confidence level (t-statistic > 2.492).

Table C.4
Individual Metal Results—Objective Equation

Metal Estimation Method	ALU 2SLS[a]	BAU 2SLS[a]	CHR 2SLS[a]	COB 2SLS[a]	COP 2SLS[a]	LEA 2SLS[a]	MAN 2SLS[a]	MOL 2SLS[a]	NIC 2SLS[a]	TIN 2SLS[a]	ZIN 2SLS[a]
Variables											
Constant	-2.41	0.33	1.18	0.17	0.85**	-0.18	1.63**	1.35***	0.03	2.04***	0.16
U.S. Agg. Econ. Activity (A1)	-0.18	-0.16	-0.45***	1.00	-0.32	0.25	-0.95***	-0.77*	-0.93*	-0.14***	0.18
U.S. Military Expenditures (A9)	0.02	-0.14	-0.14	-0.28**	-0.68**	-0.44	-0.17	-0.17	0.01*	0.18	-0.23
U.S. Import Dependence (A10)	0.17	-0.23	-0.30***	-0.48*	0.09	-0.11	-0.17***	6.70*	4.33**	-0.56	-0.46
Senators from Metal-Producing States on Key Committees (D2)	0.24	0.06*	0.14***	0.38***	0.87	0.01	-0.41	-0.03	-0.57	-0.02	-0.23
Durbin-Watson statistic	2.01	1.80	1.90	1.58	1.72	1.93	1.70	2.19	2.44	1.73	2.11
Adjusted R^2	-0.04	-0.02	0.80	0.24	0.08	-0.04	-0.22	0.07	0.02	0.40	-0.05
Rho	-0.07	0.78***	0.30***	0.77***	0.74***	0.84***	0.87***	0.77***	0.85***	0.65***	0.82***

a. Results from the 2SLS estimation with a correction for autocorrelation. (2SLS results were corrected for autocorrelation if their Durbin–Watson statistics fell outside the range between 1.78 and 2.22.)

* Coefficients are significant at the 10 percent confidence level (t-statistic > 1.318) for a one-tail test.

** Significant at the 5 percent confidence level (t-statistic > 1.711).

*** Significant at the 1 percent confidence level (t-statistic > 2.492).

Table C.5
Individual Metal Results—Inventory Change Equation

Metal Estimation Method	ALU 2SLS[a]	BAU 2SLS[a]	CHR 2SLS[a]	COB 2SLS[a]	COP 2SLS[a]	LEA 2SLS[a]	MAN 2SLS[a]	MOL 2SLS[a]	NIC 2SLS[a]	TIN 2SLS[a]	ZIN 2SLS[a]
Variables											
Constant	4.97	0.02	-0.13*	-0.11	0.01	-0.40	-0.03	0.36**	0.09	0.19**	-0.05
Senators from Metal-Producing States on Key Committees (D2)	-0.51	-0.78	0.13	0.73**	0.10	-0.25	0.35*	-0.07***	-0.01*	-0.02*	0.44**
Objective—Inventory (OI)	-2.73***	-0.04	0.13	0.03	0.05***	0.04*	0.63	-0.24**	0.02	0.05	0.08***
World Price (PN)	0.15	-0.23	0.40	0.15	-0.46*	0.48	0.31	0.31	-0.31	-0.19	-0.01*
Durbin-Watson statistic	2.00	1.90	1.98	2.92	1.80	2.01	1.96	2.07	2.14	2.00	1.80
Adjusted R²	0.49	0.27	0.05	0.07	0.12	0.02	0.04	0.25	0.24	0.98	0.23
Rho	0.068	-0.08	0.09	-0.98	0.25*	0.21*	0.24*	-0.24*	-0.36***	0.16	-0.08

a. Results from the 2SLS estimation with a correction for autocorrelation. (2SLS results were corrected for autocorrelation if their Durbin-Watson statistics fell outside the range between 1.78 and 2.22.)

* Coefficients are significant at the 10 percent confidence level (t-statistic > 1.318) for a one-tail test.

** Significant at the 5 percent confidence level (t-statistic > 1.711).

*** Significant at the 1 percent confidence level (t-statistic > 2.492).

Table C.6
Results of Pooled Estimation for U.S.-Produced Metals

Variables	Expected Sign	Total Correct Signs	No. Correct (*)	No. Correct (**)	No. Correct (***)	No. Signif.
World Price Equation						
Objective—Inventory, lagged one year (OILAG)	+	7		1	1	3
Change in Inventory (CI)	+	5		1		2
Change in Objective (CO)	+	7	1		1	2
World Agg. Econ. Activity (A2)	+	9		1	2	5
Market Concentration (A7)	+/-	11		2	1	6
GSA Price (GN)	+	8	2		1	3
Dummy for GSA purchases at Above-Market Prices (INT3)	+	6				3
Objective Equation						
U.S. Agg. Econ. Activity (A1)	+/-	11	1		3	4
U.S. Military Expenditures (A9)	+	3	1			3
U.S. Import Dependence (A10)	+	4	1	1		5
Senators from Metal-Producing States on Key Committees (D2)	+	6	1		2	3
Inventory Change Equation						
Senators from Metal-Producing Sates on Key Committees (D2)	+	5	1		2	6
Objective—Inventory (OI)	-	3		1	1	5
World Price (PN)	-	5	2			2

* Coefficients are significant at the 1 percent confidence level.

** Significant at the 5 percent confidence level.

*** Significant at the 10 percent confidence level.

Objective-Inventory in the World Price equation (3 of those were significant at least at the 10 percent confidence level). Almost the same was true for Change in Objective in this equation—7 correct signs, 2 of them significant. The sign on GSA Price was correct for 8 metals and significant for 3. The dummy variable INT3 (GSA purchases at above-market prices) showed the correct sign for 6 metals and was significant for 3 of them. The last stockpile variable, Change in Inventory, showed correct signs for 5 metals, 2 of which were significant.

In the Objective equation, the U.S. domestic political variable (D2) showed correct signs for 6 metals (significant for 3), while 4 had correct signs on U.S.

Import Dependency (2 of them significant) and 3 had correct signs on U.S. Military Expenditures (1 of them significant).

Five metals showed the expected sign for the domestic political variable in the Inventory Change equation (3 of them significant); for 3 metals, Objective-Inventory was correct in sign (significant for 2); and World Price was also correct in sign for 5 metals (significant for 2).

These results, in general, simply confirm what was reported above for the pooled estimation: stockpile variables were important predictors of world price; domestic political factors clearly mattered in the decisions concerning stockpile objectives, sales, and purchases; and stockpile inventory changes reinforced world price changes for many of the metals studied.

More interesting, however, is the question of which metals did or did not confirm the prior expectations regarding signs and importance of the variables. These comparisons can be made along several parameters, and the following sections discuss each in turn. A key distinction throughout the metal-by-metal comparisons is that between metals of which the United States was a significant producer, and those which were principally foreign-produced. The metals for which the U.S. produced at least 30 percent of its consumption, on average over the period, were aluminum, copper, lead, molybdenum, and zinc. (Aluminum, unlike the other metals on this list, was mostly produced from ores mined outside the United States—therefore, aluminum may be considered a special case, perhaps behaving more like a foreign-produced metal.)

STOCKPILE VARIABLES, WORLD PRICE, AND IMPORT DEPENDENCY

The distinction between U.S.-produced and foreign-produced metals was seen most clearly in the relationship between stockpile inventory change and world prices. While it was expected that stockpile purchases would be associated with rising prices and sales with falling prices, the opposite relationship was found for copper, lead, molybdenum, and zinc (along with several of the foreign-produced metals). In other words, stockpile sales were associated with rising prices for the four large U.S.-produced metals included in this study (and stockpile purchases accompanied falling prices.) Most of the foreign-produced metals (aluminum, bauxite, chromium, manganese, and nickel) showed the (expected) positive sign on this variable.

This result is underscored by the estimated signs on the U.S. Import Dependency variable in the stockpile Objective equation. It was expected that import dependency would be positively associated with stockpile objectives, since strategic considerations seem to imply that the larger the proportion of U.S. consumption that came from abroad, the larger the stockpiles should be. However, the estimated sign on this variable was negative for lead and zinc—along with several foreign-produced metals. This result is consistent with the evidence that despite the relatively ample domestic supplies of U.S.-produced metals, they were stock-piled in large amounts.

The results for the World Price variable in the Inventory Change equation were also consistent. World Price was negatively associated with Inventory Change for copper and zinc (both significant at the 10 percent level), plus several other metals. Again, this indicates that stockpile sales of U.S.-produced metals accompanied rising prices and stockpile sales accompanied falling prices; if stockpile purchases were used for political reasons to attempt to buttress demand for domestically produced metals during times of falling prices, this is the result that would be expected. The metals for which stockpile sales were associated with falling prices were largely the foreign-derived ones: aluminum, chromium, cobalt, and manganese.

The sign on GSA Price in the World Price equation was positive, as expected, for copper (significant at the 1 percent level) and molybdenum. It was negative, however, for lead and zinc. In other words, increases in GSA Price were associated with increases in World Price (and similarly, decreases in GSA price were associated with decreases in World Price) for two of the four U.S.-produced metals.

The Change in Objective variable was positive (as expected) in the World Price equation for 3 of the 4 U.S.-produced metals—copper (significant at the 1 percent level), lead (significant at 10 percent), and molybdenum—as well as for chromium, cobalt, manganese, and tin. Change in Objective showed a negative sign for zinc, and also for aluminum, bauxite, and nickel. This indicates that when stockpile objectives were raised, prices rose (and when objectives were lowered, prices fell) for 7 of the 11 metals, including 3 of the 4 U.S.-produced metals.

The stockpile Objective-Inventory differential had the expected (positive) sign in the Inventory Change equation for 8 of the 11 metals (4 of them significant at least at the 10 percent level). But this variable showed a negative sign for aluminum, bauxite, and molybdenum. This indicates that for those 3 metals, the GSA on average continued to buy even after the stockpile objective was met, and/or sold even when stockpile inventories were lower than objectives.

DOMESTIC POLITICAL FACTORS IN OBJECTIVE AND INVENTORY CHANGE

Variable D2 (senators from metal-producing states on key Congressional com-mittees) showed the expected positive sign in the Objective and Inventory Change equations for 2 of the 4 U.S.-produced metals. For zinc in the Inventory Change equation, variable D2 was significant at the 5 percent level. This is generally consistent with the above indications that the U.S. domestic metals industries were successful at increasing stockpile objectives and inventories in their favor. However, the expectation that this variable would be more significant for domes-tically produced metals than for foreign ones was not borne out. Of the 9 metals for which variable D2 was significant in the Objective and Inventory Change equations, only 1 (molybdenum) was domestically produced. Since the domestic political variable was significant in the pooled estimation, these results are somewhat surprising. Possibly they are partially due to the sorts of cross-metal substitution and complementarity effects noted in chapter 2.

CONCLUSION

Simultaneous estimations of the four-equation model generally confirmed that stockpile variables were significant influences upon world metal price changes. Many of the expected differences between U.S.-produced and foreign-derived metals were apparent in the individual metal estimations of the model. Several other hypotheses concerning the effects of differentials between the GSA price and the market price, domestic and foreign political factors, market concentration, and the interrelationships among the various stockpile variables were also satisfactorily tested.

NOTES

1. Johnson and Rausser, 758.
2. Federal Emergency Management Agency, "Methodology of Estimating Stockpile Goals," 1976.
3. The variables, which are, for simplicity, denoted A1 through A10, are all series of statistics that are relevant to metals markets, but not all of these variables appear in the final model. Some are instruments that are used to calculate other variables. For example, variable A10 (U.S. import dependency) was derived by subtracting variable A5 (U.S. production) from variable A6 (U.S. consumption).
4. An alternative way to proxy the resource demand effects and inflation that accompany military conflicts is an index developed by Singer and Small (J. D. Singer and M. Small, *The Wages of War*, New York: John Wiley, 1972, 210–11), of the "annual nation-months of wars underway, normalized by system size." Although the Singer and Small index includes conflicts that did not directly involve the United States, presumably the resource demands made by any war would affect world metals markets, prices, and stockpile policy makers' decisions. The Singer and Small index is denoted variable A3 and tested in the model interchangeably with variable A9, U.S. military expenditures. Theoretically, either A3 or A9, but not both, may reasonably be included in the O equation. The Singer and Small index is not available after the mid-1970s, so variable A9 is used in testing the full model.
5. See discussion in Barry R. Weingast and Mark J. Moran, "Bureaucratic Discretion or Congressional Control?," *Journal of Political Economy* 91 (1983): 765–800, of the literature on why and how this congruence occurs.
6. See Real P. Lavergne, *The Political Economy of U.S. Tariffs* (Toronto: Academic Press, 1983), 3–4.
7. See Robert Axelrod, *The Evolution of Cooperation* (New York: Basic Books, 1984), 16.
8. One expectation which should generally hold for all the variables measuring domestic political factors is that they would prove to be of greater significance for metals

that the United States produced domestically than for metals that were not produced in the United States to any great extent.

9. These changes included dropping variable A2 from the Objective equation and variable A1 from the World Price equation as these two variables were closely correlated, and dropping three variables—I/A4, INT1, and MCOMP—from the World Price equation because they proved to be insignificant. Variable I/A4 (inventory as a proportion of world production) was intended to capture the effect of the stockpile's "hanging over" world price; it appears that this effect is not a significant one for the eleven metals in the aggregate. The insignificance of the variable MCOMP in the World Price equation indicates that interactions between the aluminum and bauxite markets were not an important factor affecting world price for these commodities. The insignificance of variable INT1 (the dummy variable designed to test whether the interaction between U.S.-produced metals and inventory change had a large effect on price) seems to indicate that U.S.-produced metals are no more likely than other metals to be associated with price effects linked to inventory change.

In the Objective equation and the Inventory Change equation, variable F1 (U.S. exports to metal-producing countries) proved insignificant, and it was therefore dropped. This indicates that foreign policy considerations, insofar as they are proxied by F1, were relatively unimportant in stockpile decision making.

On theoretical grounds, the two domestic political variables (D1 and D2)—which were both proxies for the same influences on stockpile policy making—should not both be included in the Objective and Inventory Change equations. They were highly correlated. Not surprisingly, variable D2 (senators from metal-producing states on key Congressional committees) predicted better than D1 (population of metal-producing states) in both equations, so it was used throughout.

10. For example, normalized price ranges over the early part of the period for the eleven metals ranged from the level of $0.00017–$0.00033 per short ton for bauxite, to $4.15–$6.96 per short ton for manganese, although seven of the metals ranged entirely between $0.02 and $1.41 per short ton.

Bibliography

Adams, F. Gerard. "Modeling of the World Commodity Markets: Perspectives on the Use of Commodity Market Models for Forecasting and Simulation." In *World Bank Commodity Models*, World Bank Staff Commodity Working Paper, Vol. 1, No. 6, 1981.

————. *The Impact of Cobalt Production from the Ocean Floor.* Study prepared for UNCTAD. Philadelphia: Wharton School, 1972.

Adams, F. Gerard, et al. *An Econometric Analysis of International Trade.* Paris: OECD, 1969.

Adams, F. Gerard and J. R. Behrman. *Econometric Modeling of World Commodity Policy.* Lexington, MA: Lexington Books, 1978.

Adams, F. Gerard and S. A. Klein, eds. *Stabilizing World Commodity Markets.* Lexington, MA: Heath, 1978.

Agarwal, J. C. and B. J. Reddy. *Role of Cobalt in Industrial Society.* Boston: Charles River Associates, 1980.

Agbeyegbe, Terence D. "Interest Rates and Metal Price Movements: Further Evidence." *Journal of Environmental Economics and Management* 16 (1989): 184–92.

Ali, Liaqat. "Principle of Buffer Stock and its Mechanism in the International Tin Agreement." *Weltwirtschaftliches Archiv* 96 (1966): 141–87.

Allingham, M. and C. L. Gilbert. "Economic Modeling of the Mineral Sector with Reference to Commmodity Agreements." In *Application of Computer Methods in the Mineral Industry*, edited by R.V. Ramani. New York: Society of Mining Engineers of the American Institute of Mining, Metallurgical, and Petroleum Engineers, Inc., 1977.

American Bureau of Metal Statistics. *Non-Ferrous Metal Data.* New York, published annually.

Anam, Mahmudal. "Distortion-Triggered Lobbying and Welfare." *Journal of International Economics* 13 (August 1982): 15–32.

Anderson, Ewan W. *The Structure and Dynamics of U.S. Government Policymaking: The Case of Strategic Minerals.* New York: Praeger, 1988.

Askari, Hossain and G. Weil. "Stability of Export Earnings of Developing Nations." *Journal of Development Studies* 11, no. 1 (1974): 86–90.

Auty, Richard M. *Sustaining Development in Mineral Economies: The Resource Curse Thesis.* London/New York: Routledge, 1993.

————. "Multinational Corporations and Regional Revenue Retention in a Vertically Integrated Industry: Bauxite/Aluminum in the Caribbean." *Regional Studies* 17, no. 1 (February 1983): 3–17.

Axelrod, Robert. *The Evolution of Cooperation.* New York: Basic Books, 1984.

Baldwin, R. E. and A. O. Krueger. *The Structure and Evolution of Recent U.S. Trade Policy.* Chicago: University of Chicago Press, 1984.

Baldwin, William L. *The World Tin Market: Political Pricing and Economic Competition.* Durham, NC: Duke University Press, 1983.

Banks, Ferdinand E. *Bauxite and Aluminum: An Introduction to the Economics of Nonfuel Minerals.* Lexington, MA: Lexington Books, 1979.

————. *The World Copper Market: An Economic Analysis.* Cambridge: Ballinger, 1974.

————. "An Econometric Model of the World Tin Economy: A Comment." *Econometrica* 40, no. 4 (July 1972): 749–52.

Barham, Bradford, Stephen G. Bunker and Denis O'Hearn, eds. *States, Firms, and Raw Materials: The World Economy and Ecology of Aluminum.* Madison, Wisconsin: University of Wisconsin Press, 1994.

Bedregal, Guillermo. *El Convenio Internacional del Estaño.* La Paz: Corporación Minera de Bolivia, 1962.

Behrman, Jere R. "International Commodity Market Structures and the Theory Underlying International Commodity Market Models." In *Econometric Modeling of World Commodity Policy*, edited by F. G. Adams and J. R. Behrman. Lexington, MA: Lexington, Books, 1978.

Behrman, Jere R. and P. Tinakorn. "The Impact of the UNCTAD Integrated Programme on Latin American Export Earnings." In *Commodity Markets and Latin American Development: A Modeling Approach*, edited by M. Labys et al. Cambridge: Ballinger, 1980.

Bencivenga, Valerie R. "An Econometric Model of the Geographical Distribution of Foreign Aid." Ph.D. Thesis, University of Toronto, 1984.

Bennett, Harold J., J. G. Thompson and G.A. Kingston. "A Systematic Approach to the Appraisal of National Mineral Supply." In *Application of Computer Methods in the Mineral Industry,* edited by R. V. Ramani. New York: Society of Mining Engineers of the American Institute of Mining, Metallurgical, and Petroleum Engineers, Inc., 1977.

Bennett, James T. and W. E. Williams. *Strategic Minerals: The Economic Impact of Supply Disruptions.* Washington, DC: Heritage Foundation, 1981.

Bennett, M. K. and Associates. *International Commodity Stockpiling as an Economic Stabilizer.* Stanford: Stanford University Press, 1949.

Berger, Alan H. "Commodity Markets: Nickel and Cobalt." *Journal of Metals* 30, no. 4 (April 1978): 10–11.

Bergesen, Albert, ed. "Cycles of War in the Reproduction of the World Economy." In *Rhythms in Politics and Economics*, edited by P.M. Johnson and W.R. Thompson. New York: Praeger, 1985.

————. "Modeling Long Waves of Crisis in the World-System." In *Crises in the World-System*, edited by A. Bergesen. Beverly Hills, CA: Sage, 1983.

————. *Crisis in the World-System.* Beverly Hills, CA: Sage, 1983.

Bergsten, C. F. "One, Two, Many OPECs ...? The Threat is Real." *Foreign Policy* 14 (Spring 1974): 84–90.

————. "The Threat from the Third World." *Foreign Policy* 11 (Summer 1973): 102–24.

Bomsel, Olivier and Christian von Hirschhausen. "The Metal Mining Industry in Eastern Europe: Its Difficult Reconversion and Future Impact on World Markets." *Natural Resources Forum* (November 1992): 250–60.

Bosson, R. and B. Varon. *The Mining Industry and the Developing Countries*. New York: Oxford University Press, 1977.

Brock, W. A. and S. P. Magee. "The Economics of Special Interest Politics: The Case of the Tariff." *American Economic Review* 68, no. 2 (May 1978): 246–50.

Brookings Institution. *Trade in Primary Commodities: Conflict or Cooperation?* Washington, DC: Brookings Institution, 1974.

Brown, C. P. *Primary Commodity Control*. Kuala Lumpur: Oxford University Press, 1975.

Brown, Martin S. and J. Butler. *The Production, Marketing and Consumption of Copper and Aluminum*. New York: Praeger, 1968.

Bullis, L. Harold and J. E. Mielke. *Strategic and Critical Materials*. Boulder, CO: Westview, 1985.

Burrows, James C. *Cobalt: An Industry Analysis*. Lexington, MA: Lexington Books, 1971.

————. *Tungsten: An Industry Analysis*. Lexington, MA: Lexington Books, 1971.

"By All Means ... Let's Have the Facts about Stockpiling." *Engineering and Mining Journal* (March 1962): 4, 73.

Cameron Eugene N. *At the Crossroads: The Mineral Problems of the U.S.* New York: Wiley, 1986.

————. *The Mineral Position of the U.S., 1975-2000*. Madison: University of Wisconsin Press, 1973.

Campbell, Gary A. "Disequilibrium Effects on Metal Demand Estimation: A Study of Cobalt Demand." *Materials and Society* 7, no. 2 (1983): 163–71.

Cardoso, Fernando Henrique. "Challenge to Models: How Can Patterns of International Dependence and Participation be Quantified and Simulated?" In *Problems of World Modeling*, edited by K. W. Deutsch, et al. Cambridge: Ballinger, 1977.

Charette, Michael F. "Determinants of Export Instability in the Primary Commodity Trade of Less-Developed Countries." *Journal of Development Economics* 18 (1985): 13–21.

Chhabra, J.E., J. E. Grilli, and P. Pollak. *The World Tin Economy: An Econometric Analysis*. World Bank Staff Commodity Paper No. 1. Washington, DC: World Bank, 1978.

Choksi, Shernaz. "Aluminum Price Behavior: A Decade on the LME." *Resources Policy* 17, no. 1 (March 1991): 13–21.

Chung, Julius C. "U.S. Chromium Market: An Econometric Presentation." *Resources Policy* 13, no. 3 (September 1987): 207–27.

Collins, Elizabeth. "Primary Metals Cartels: Few Could Match the Success of OPEC." *Metals and Materials* (March 1977): 38–39.

"Commodities: On a War Footing." *The Economist* (February 1983): 83–84.

Commodity Research Bureau. *Commodity Year Book*. Jersey City, NJ: Commodity Research Bureau, Inc., annual.

Commodity Research Unit Ltd. *Coordinated National Stockpiles as a Market Stabilizing Mechanism: Copper*. London: Commodity Research Unit Ltd., 1977.

"Congress Bars Imports of Rhodesian Chrome." *Chemical and Engineering News* 21 (March 1977): 8.

Copulos, Milton R. *Securing America's Energy and Mineral Needs*. Washington, DC: The Heritage Foundation, 1989.

Cornell, Robert A. "United States Stockpile Policy." Paper presented at the American Mining Congress Mining Convention, Los Angeles, September 23–26, 1979 (mimeo).

Cuddy, John D. A. "Theory and Practice in NIEO Negotiations on Commodities." In *For Good or Evil*, edited by G. K. Helleiner. Toronto: University of Toronto Press, 1982.

Cunningham, S. *The Copper Industry in Zambia*. New York: Praeger, 1981.

Curlee, T. Randall and Sujit Das. "Advanced Materials: Information and Analysis Needs." *Resources Policy* 17, no. 4 (December 1991): 316–31.

Dammert, Alfredo J. and Jasbir G. S. Chhabra. *The Lead and Zinc Industries: Long-Term Prospects*. World Bank Commodity Working Paper No. 22. Washington, DC: World Bank, 1990.

De Sa, Paulo. "The European Non-ferrous Metals Industry: 1993 and Beyond." *Resources Policy* 17, no. 3 (September 1991): 211–25.

"Defence Stockpile." *Globe and Mail* (March 1981), Toronto.

DeMille, John B. *Strategic Minerals*. New York: McGraw-Hill, 1947.

Denoon, David B.H. *The New International Economic Order: A U.S. Response*. London: Macmillan, 1980.

Desai, Meghnad. "An Econometric Model of the World Tin Economy, 1948–1961." *Econometrica* 34, no. 1 (January 1966): 105–34.

Deutsch, Karl W., et al., eds. *Problems of World Modeling: Political and Social Implications*. Cambridge: Ballinger, 1977.

Deverell, John. *Falconbridge*. Toronto: Lorimer, 1970.

Dobney, Frederick J. "Stockpiling and Shortages." *Social Science Quarterly* 57 (Spring 1976): 455–65.

Dobozi, Istvan. "State Enterprises, Supply Behavior and Market Volatility: An Empirical Analysis of the World Copper Industry." *Resources Policy* 19, no. 1 (March 1993): 40–50.

Doran, Charles F. "Power Cycle Theory and Systems Stability." In *Rhythms in Politics and Economics*, edited by Paul M. Johnson and W. R. Thompson. New York: Praeger, 1985.

———. "Change, Uncertainty, and Balance: A Dynamic View of U.S. Foreign Policy." *International Journal* 35, no. 3 (Summer 1980): 563–79.

Doran, Charles F. and Wes Parsons. "War and the Cycle of Relative Power." *American Political Science Review* 74, no. 4 (December 1980): 947–65.

Dybalski, G. "An Economic Model of the Cobalt Market." Presented at the XIV Symposium of the Council for the Application of Computers and Mathematics in the Minerals Industry, University Park, PA, 1976.

Eaton, Jonathan and Zvi Eckstein. "The U.S. Strategic Petroleum Reserve: An Analytic Framework." In *The Structure and Evolution of Recent U.S. Trade Policy*, edited by R. E. Baldwin and A. O. Krueger. Chicago: University of Chicago Press, 1984.

Eckes, Jr., A. E. *The U.S. and the Global Struggle for Minerals*. Austin: University of Texas, 1979.

Elder, Robert E. and Jack E. Holmes. "International Economic Long Cycles and American Foreign Policy Moods." In *Rhythms in Politics and Economics*, edited by Paul M. Johnson and W. R. Thompson. New York: Praeger, 1985.

Faber, M. L. O. and J. G. Potter. *Towards Economic Independence: Papers on the Nationalization of the Copper Industry in Zambia*. Cambridge: Cambridge University Press, 1971.

Falconer, R. T. and C. M. Sivesind. "Dealing with Conflicting Forecasts: The Eclectic Advantage." *Business Economics* 10 (1977): 5–11.

Federal Emergency Management Agency. "Methodology of Estimating Stockpile Goals." Washington, DC: Federal Emergency Management Agency, 1976 (mimeo).
————. *Stockpile Report to the Congress*. Washington, DC: Federal Emergency Management Agency, various years.
Fine, Daniel I. "The Big U.S. Stake in South Africa's Minerals." *Business Week* (January 29, 1979): 55.
Finger, J. M., H. K. Hall, and D. R. Nelson. "The Political Economy of Administered Protection." *American Economic Review* 72, no. 3 (June 1982): 452–66.
Fischman, Leonard L., ed. *World Mineral Trends and U.S. Supply Problems*. Washington, DC: Resources for the Future, 1980.
Fisher, F. M., P. H. Cootner and M. N. Baily. "An Economic Model of the World Copper Industry." *Bell Journal of Economics* 3, no. 2 (Autumn 1972): 568–609.
Fisher, Richard W. and R. V. Roosa. "An Alternative Common Fund Proposal." In *Stabilizing World Commodity Markets*, edited by F. G. Adams and S. A. Klein. Lexington, MA: Heath, 1978.
Fortin, C. "Third World Commodity Policy at the Crossroads: Some Fundamental Issues." *IFDA Dossier* 15 (January–February 1980).
Fox, William. *Tin: The Working of a Commodity Agreement*. London: Mining Journal Books, 1974.
French, M. W. "Should Policymaking Account for Market Expectations? An Estimate of Their Impact on Commodity Policy." *Journal of Policy Modeling* 4, no. 2 (1982): 243–58.
Frey, Bruno. S. "The Public Choice View of International Political Economy." *International Organization* 38, no. 1 (Winter 1984): 199–23.
Fried, Edward R. "International Trade in Raw Materials: Myths and Realities." *Science*, 191 (1976): 641–46.
Friedland, Jonathan. "Struggling Producers Lay Siege to Washington's Hoard." *South* (May 1983): 72–73.
Gauntt, Gerald E. "Market Stabilization and the Strategic Stockpile." *Materials and Society* 4 (1980): 203–9.
Gedicks, Al. *The New Resource Wars: Native and Environmental Struggles Against Multinational Corporations*. Montreal: Black Rose Books, 1994.
Geer, T. "The Postwar Tin Agreements: A Case of Success in Price Stabilization of Primary Commodities?" *Revue Suisse d'Economie Politique et de Statistique*" 2 (1970): 189–236.
Glezakos, Constantine. "Instability and the Growth of Exports." *Journal of Development Economics* 12 (1983): 229–36.
Gocht, Werner, H. Zantop and R. G. Eggert. *International Mineral Economics: Mineral Exploration, Mine Valuation, Mineral Markets, International Mineral Policies*. Berlin: Springer, 1988.
Gordon-Ashworth, Fiona. *International Commodity Control*. London: Croom Helm, 1984.
"GSA's Mineral Deposit." *The Economist*, July 21, 1979.
Gupta, Poonam and Sanjeev Gupta. "World Demand for Cobalt: An Econometric Study." *Resources Policy* 9, no. 4 (December 1983): 261–74.
Gupta, Satyadev. *The World Zinc Industry*. Lexington, MA: Lexington Books, 1982.
Guvenen, O., W. C. Labys, and J.-S. Lesourd. *International Commodity Market Models: Advances in Methodology and Applications*. London: Chapman and Hall, 1991.
Haglund, David G., ed. *The New Geopolitics of Minerals: Canada and International Resource Trade*. Vancouver: University of British Columbia Press, 1989.

Haglund, David G. "The New Geopolitics of Minerals: An Inquiry into the Changing International Significance of Strategic Minerals." *Political Geography Quarterly* 5 (July 1986): 221–40.

———. "Strategic Minerals: A Conceptual Analysis." *Resources Policy* 10, no. 3 (September 1984): 146–52.

Hallwood, Paul. "Interaction Between Private Speculation and Buffer Stock Agencies in Commodity Stabilization." *World Development* 5, no. 4 (1977): 349–53.

Handler, Edward and J. R. Mulkern. *Business in Politics*. Lexington, MA: Lexington Books, 1982.

Hardin, Russell. *Collective Action*. Baltimore: Johns Hopkins University Press, 1982.

Hargreaves, David and S. Fromson. *World Index of Strategic Minerals: Production, Exploitation and Risk*. New York: Facts on File, 1983.

Harris, Stuart, M. Salmon, and B. Smith. *Analysis of Commodity Markets of Policy Purposes*. Thames Essays No. 17. London: Trade Policy Research Centre, 1978.

Harrison, M. "Strategic Metals Hit by Cuts." *Engineer* 1–8 (December 1983): 7–8.

Hashimoto, Hideo. *A Tin Economy Model for Decision Making about Investment in Production Capacity*. London: International Tin Council, 1981.

Helleiner, G. K. *For Good or Evil*. Toronto: University of Toronto Press, 1982.

———. "Freedom and Management in Primary Commodity Markets: U.S. Imports from Developing Countries." *World Development* 6, no. 1 (January 1978): 23–30.

———. "Transnational Enterprises and the New Political Economy of U.S. Trade Policy." *Oxford Economic Papers* 29, no. 1 (March 1977): 102–16.

Helpman, Elhanan. "A Simple Theory of International Trade with Multinational Corporations." *Journal of Political Economy* 92, no. 3 (1984): 451–71.

Hersh, Seymour M. "The Wild East." *Atlantic Monthly* 273, no. 6 (June 1994): 61–86.

Hickey, John. "The Stabilization Program of the U.S. in Jamaica." *Inter-American Economic Affairs* 37 (Autumn 1983): 63–72.

Hilmy, J. *"Old Nick"—An Anatomy of the Nickel Industry and its Future*. World Bank Commodity Note No. 13. Washington, DC: World Bank, 1979.

"Hoarding Helps, Provided Minerals are Stockpiled Slowly—and Cheaply." *The Economist* 271 (June 2, 1979): 84–85.

Hoselitz, Bert F. "International Cartel Policy." *Journal of Political Economy* 55, no. 1 (February 1947): 1–27.

Hufbauer, G. C. and J. J. Schott. *Economic Sanctions in Support of Foreign Policy Goals*. Washington: Institute for International Economics, 1983.

Hughes, Helen. "Economic Rents, the Distribution of Gains from Mineral Exploitation, and Mineral Development Policy." *World Development* 3, nos. 11–12 (1975): 811–25.

Humphreys, David. "Similarities and Differences in the Economics of Metals and Industrial Minerals." *Resources Policy* 17, no. 3 (September 1991): 184–94.

Hveem, Helge. "Militarization of Nature: Conflict and Control Over Strategic Resources and Some Implications for Peace Policies." *Journal of Peace Research* 16, no. 1 (1979).

———. *The Political Economy of Third World Producer Associations*. International Peace Research Institute Monographs, no. 6. Oslo: Universitetsforlaget, 1978.

Hwa, Erh-Cheng. *A Simultaneous Equation Model of Price and Quantity Adjustments in Primary Commodity Markets*. World Bank Staff Working Paper No. 499. Washington, DC: World Bank, October 1981.

"In Prospect: Stockpiling Goods to Curb Price Boosts." *U.S. News and World Report* (April 18, 1977): 86.

International Economic Studies Institute. *Raw Materials and Foreign Policy*. Washington, DC: International Economic Studies Institute, 1976.

International Institute for Peace and Related Research. *SIPRI Yearbook of World Armaments and Disarmaments*. Stockholm International Peace Research Institute. First published 1968.

International Institute for Strategic Studies. *The Military Balance*. Published annually since 1965.

International Tin Council. *Fourth World Conference on Tin, Kuala Lumpur, 1974*. London: ITC, 1974.

————. *The International Implications of U.S. Disposal of Stockpiled Tin*. London: ITC, 1973.

————. *Conference on Tin Consumption*. London: ITC and Tin Research Institute, 1972.

Ip, Greg. "Resource Firms Face Grim Reality." *The Financial Post* (July 10, 1993).

Jacobson, D. M., R. K. Turner, and A. A. L. Challis. "A Reassessment of the Strategic Materials Question." *Resources Policy* 14, no. 2 (June 1988): 74–84.

Johnson, S. R. and G. C. Rausser. "Composite Forecasting in Commodity Systems." In *New Directions in Econometric Modeling and Forecasting in U.S. Agriculture*, edited by G. C. Rausser. New York: Elsevier, 1982.

Jordan, Amos A. and R. A. Kilmarx. *Strategic Mineral Dependence: The Stockpile Dilemma*. Beverly Hills, CA: Sage Publications, 1979.

Just, Richard E. and J. A. Hallah. "New Developments in Econometric Valuations of Price Stabilizing and Destabilizing Policies." In *New Directions in Econometric Modeling and Forecasting in U.S. Agriculture*, edited by G. C. Rausser. New York: Elsevier, 1982.

Kaldor, N. "The Role of Commodity Prices in Economic Recovery." *Lloyd's Bank Review* 149 (July 1983): 21–34.

Kenen, P. and V. C. Voivodas. "Export Instability and Economic Growth." *Kyklos* 25 (1972): 791–804.

Keynes, J. M. *Some Aspects of Commodity Markets*. Manchester Guardian Commercial: European Reconstruction Series, March 29, 1923.

Klass, M. W., et al. *International Minerals Cartels and Embargoes: Policy Implications for the U.S.* New York: Praeger, 1980.

Klein, Lawrence R. "Potentials of Econometrics for Commodity Stabilization Policy Analysis." In *Stabilizing World Commodity Markets*, edited by F. G. Adams and S. Klein. Lexington, MA: Heath, 1978.

Kline, John M. *State Government Influence in United States International Economic Policy*. Lexington, MA: Lexington Books, 1983.

Knorr, K. E. *Tin Under Control*. Stanford, CA: Food Research Institute, 1945.

Kostecki, M. M., ed. *The Soviet Impact on Commodity Markets*. New York: St. Martin's, 1984.

————. *State Trading in International Markets*. New York: St. Martin's, 1982.

Krasner, Stephen D. "State Power and the Structure of International Trade." *World Politics* 28, no. 3 (April 1976): 317–47.

————. "One, Two, Many OPECs ...? Oil is the Exception." *Foreign Policy* 14 (Spring 1974): 68–84.

Krueger, Paul K. "Modeling Future Requirements for Metals and Minerals." In *Application of Computer Methods in the Mineral Industry*, edited by R. V. Ramani. New York: Society of Mining Engineers of the American Institute of Mining, Metallurgical, and Petroleum Engineers, Inc., 1977.

Kudrle, R. T. "The Political Economy of U.S. Protectionism." In *Rhythms in Politics and Economics*, edited by Paul M. Johnson and W. R. Thompson. New York: Praeger Scientific, 1985.

Labys, Walter C. *Primary Commodity Markets and Models*. Aldershot, Hants: Gower, 1987.

———. "Commodity Price Stabilization Models: A Review and Appraisal." *Journal of Policy Modeling* 2, no. 1 (1980): 121–36.

———. *Market Structure, Bargaining Power, and Resource Price Formation*. Lexington, MA: Heath, 1980.

———. "Commodity Markets and Models: The Range of Experience." In *Stabilizing World Commodity Markets*, edited by F. G. Adams and S. Klein. Lexington, MA: Heath, 1978.

———. *Quantitative Models of Commodity Markets*. Cambridge: Ballinger, 1975.

Labys, Walter C. and C. W. J. Granger. *Speculation, Hedging and Commodity Price Forecasts*. Lexington, MA: Heath, 1970.

Labys, Walter C., M. I. Nadiri and J. N. del Arco. *Commodity Markets and Latin American Economic Development: A Modeling Approach*. Cambridge: Ballinger, 1980.

Labys, Walter C. and H. Thomas. "Speculation, Hedging and Commodity Price Behavior: An International Comparison." *Applied Economics* 7 (1975): 287–301.

Lanning, Greg and M. Mueller. *Africa Undermined*. Harmondsworth: Penguin, 1979.

Laursen, Karsten and Ebbe Yndgaard. "Issues in Commodity Model Building: Summary Discussion." In *World Bank Commodity Models*. World Bank Staff Commodity Working Paper 1, no. 6 (1981).

Lavergne, Real P. *The Political Economy of U.S. Tariffs*. Toronto: Academic Press, 1983.

Lavite, M. M. "Marketing in a Cyclical Business: Lessons from the Molybdenum Industry." *Resources Policy* 17, no. 2 (June 1991): 149–57.

Lax, Marc D. *Selected Strategic Minerals: The Impending Crisis*. Lanham, MD/New York/London: University Press of America, 1992.

Lee, Elizabeth Carol. "Bauxite for Butter: The Implications of the Agreement with Jamaica to Trade Surplus Agriculture Products for Strategic Materials, 1950–1967." *Law and Policy in International Business* 16, no. 1 (1984): 239–61.

Lee Seon and D. Blandford. "Price vs. Revenue Stabilization Through a Buffer Stock: Which Is More Financially Feasible for LDCs?" *Journal of Policy Modeling* 3, no. 2 (May 1981): 245–50.

Leontief, Wassily, James C. M. Koo, S. Nasar, and I. Sohn. *The Future of Nonfuel Minerals in the U.S. and World Economy*. Lexington, MA: Lexington Books, 1983.

Levitan, Sar A. and Martha R. Cooper. *Business Lobbies: The Public Good and the Bottom Line*. Baltimore: Johns Hopkins University Press, 1984.

Lord, Montague J. "Distributional Effects of International Commodity Price Stabilization: Do the Aggregate Gains Apply to Individual Producing Countries?" *Journal of Policy Modeling* 3, no. 1 (1981): 61–75.

Lovering, Thomas S. *Minerals in World Affairs*. New York: Prentice Hall, 1943.

MacAvoy, Paul. *Explaining Metals Prices: Economic Analysis of Metals Markets in the 1980s and 1990s*. Boston: Kluwer, 1988.

Macbean, Alasdair. *Export Instability and Economic Development*. London: Allen and Unwin, 1966.

MacKinnon, J. G. and N. D. Olewiler. "Disequilibrium Estimate of the Price for Copper." *Bell Journal of Economics* 11 (1980): 197–211.

Magdoff, Harry. "Militarism and Imperialism." *American Economic Review* 60, no. 2 (May 1970): 237–42.

Mangone, Gerard J., ed. *American Strategic Minerals.* New York: Crane Russak, 1984.

Mardones, Jose Luis, Enrique Silva, and Cristian Martínez. "The Copper and Aluminum Industries: A Review of Structural Changes." *Resources Policy* 11, no. 1 (March 1985): 3–16.

"A Market Ripe for Manipulation: Laxity in London Opened Door for a Sumitomo Trader." *The New York Times* (July 12, 1996): C1.

Marsden, R. *Politics, Minerals, and Survival.* Madison: University of Wisconsin Press, 1975.

Marshall, Isabel, Enrique Silva, and Alfonso Gonzalez. "The Competitive Strategy of Codelco and Other Leading Copper Producers: Changes during the Last Decade." *Resources Policy* 19, no. 2 (June 1993): 90–97.

McClelland, Peter. *Causal Explanation and Model Building in History, Economics, and the New Economic History.* Ithaca, NY: Cornell University Press, 1975.

McClure, James A. "Stockpiling of Strategic and Critical Materials." *Idaho Law Review* 19 (1983): 417–53.

McFadden, Eric J. "The Collapse of Tin: Restructuring a Failed Commodity Agreement." *American Journal of International Law* 80 (October 1986): 811–30.

McKinnon, Ronald I. "Futures Markets, Buffer Stocks, and Income Stability for Primary Producers." *Journal of Political Economy* 75, no. 6 (1967): 844–61.

McNicol, D. L. *Commodity Agreements and Price Stabilization.* Lexington, MA: Heath, 1978.

Meadows, D. L., et al. *Limits to Growth.* New York: Universe, 1972.

Mellow, Craig. "The Metals Queen of Tallinn." *Forbes* (December 21, 1992): 42–44.

"Metal Contract Revision Saves Government Millions." *American Metal Market* 6 (January 1959): 9.

Meyer, Herbert E. "Russia's Sudden Reach for Raw Materials." *Fortune* 102 (July 28, 1980): 43–44.

Mikesell, Raymond F. *Nonfuel Minerals: Foreign Dependence and National Security.* Ann Arbor: University of Michigan Press, 1987.

———. *Stockpiling Strategic Materials: An Evaluation of the National Program.* Washington, DC: American Enterprise Institute, 1986.

———. *The World Copper Industry.* Baltimore: Johns Hopkins Press, 1979.

"Mining Woes Blamed on Politics." *Toronto Star* (March 30, 1993).

Mizzi, Philip J., S. C. Maurice, and G. Anders. "The Nickel Industry: Continued Response to a Changing Environment." *Resources Policy* 13, no. 1 (March 1987): 35–46.

Mo, William Y. "A Mathematical Model for the Determination of an Optimal Stockpile to Counteract Foreign-Induced Commodity Actions." In *Application of Computer Methods in the Mineral Industry,* edited by R. V. Ramani. New York: Society of Mining Engineers of the American Institute of Mining, Metallurgical, and Petroleum Engineers, Inc., 1977.

Modelski, George. "The Long Cycle of Global Politics and the Nation-State." *Comparative Studies in Society and History* 20 (April 1978): 214–35.

———. "Dependency Reversal in the Modern State System: A Long Cycle Perspective." In *North/South Relations,* edited by G. Modelski, C. F. Doran, and C. Clark. New York: Praeger, 1983.

Molybdenum Production in the 20th Century. Santiago: Alexander Sutulov, 1980.

Muñoz, Heraldo. "Strategic Dependency and Foreign Policy: Notes on the Relations Between Core Powers and Mineral-Exporting Periphery Countries." *Vierteljahresberichte* (June 1980): 165–80.

Murray, D. "Export Earnings Instability: Price, Quantity, Supply, Demand?" *Economic Development and Cultural Change 27*, no. 1 (October 1978): 61–73.

"Mysterious Buyers with an Insatiable Lust for Tin." *Economist* 282 (January 23, 1982): 57–58.

Nappi, Carmine. *Metals Demand and the Canadian Metal Industry: Structural Changes and Policy Implications*. Kingston, Ontario: Queens University Centre for Resource Studies, 1989.

———. "Pricing Behavior and Market Power in North American Non-Ferrous Metal Industries." *Resources Policy 11*, no. 3 (September 1985): 213–24.

———. *Commodity Market Controls: A Historical Review*. Lexington, MA: Lexington Books, 1979.

Netschert, Bruce C. "U.S. Dependence on Imported Nonfuel Minerals: The Threat of Mini-OPECs?" *Journal of Metals* (March 1981): 31–38.

Newbery, D. M. "Commodity Price Stabilization in Imperfect or Cartelized Markets." *Econometrica* 52 (1984): 563–78.

Newbery, D. M. G. and J. E. Stiglitz. *The Theory of Commodity Price Stabilization: A Study in the Economics of Risk*. New York: Oxford University Press, 1981.

Nichols, Albert L. and R. J. Zeckhauser. "Stockpiling Strategies and Cartel Prices." *Bell Journal of Economics 8*, no. 1 (Spring 1977): 66–96.

Nwoke, Chibuzo. *Third World Minerals and Global Pricing*. London and New Jersey: Zed Books, 1987.

Nziramasanga, M. T. and C. Obidegwu. "Primary Commodity Price Fluctuations and Developing Countries: An Econometric Model of Copper and Zambia." *Journal of Development Economics 9*, no. 1 (August 1981): 89–119.

Odell, J. S. "Latin American Trade Negotiations with the U.S." *International Organization 34* (Spring 1980): 207–28.

Ogunbadejo, Oye. *The International Politics of Africa's Strategic Minerals*. Westport, CT: Greenwood Press, 1985.

Ophuls, W. "The Scarcity Society." *Harper's Magazine* 248, no. 1487 (April 1974): 47–52.

Organization for Economic Cooperation and Development. *Resolution of the Council Concerning the Declaration on Risk Reduction for Lead*. Paris: OECD, March 21, 1996. Document C(96)42/FINAL.

"Ottawa Considers Sale of Uranium." *Globe and Mail* (October 12, 1979), Toronto.

Page, W. and H. Rush. *Long Term Forecasts for Metals: The Track Record, 1910–1960s*. Science Policy Research Unit, University of Sussex, U.K., April 1978.

Pastor, Robert. *Congress and the Politics of U.S. Foreign Economic Policy, 1929–1976*. Berkeley: University of California Press, 1980.

Pearson, S. and J. Cownie, eds. *Commodity Exports and African Economic Development*. Lexington, MA: Heath, 1974.

Peck, Merton J., ed. *The World Aluminum Industry in a Changing Energy Era*. Washington, DC: Resources for the Future, 1988.

Peters, Charles. *How Washington Really Works*. Reading, MA: Addison Wesley, 1980.

Petras, James F. and M. H. Morley. *How Allende Fell*. Nottingham: Spokesman Books, 1974.

Pincus, J. J. "Pressure Groups and the Pattern of Tariffs." *Journal of Political Economy 83*, no. 4 (1975): 757–78.

Pindyck, Robert S. "Gains to Producers from the Cartelization of Exhaustible Resources." *Review of Economics and Statistics* 60, no. 2 (1978): 238–51.

―――. "Cartel Pricing and the Structure of the World Bauxite Market." *Bell Journal of Economics* (Autumn 1977): 343–60.

Ponting, Clive. *A Green History of the World.* New York: Penguin, 1991.

Preeg, Ernest H. *Traders and Diplomats: An Analysis of the Kennedy Round of Negotiations under the GATT.* Washington, DC: Brookings Institution, 1970.

Prest, Michael. "The Collapse of the International Tin Agreement: The Consequences." *Round Table* (April 1987): 167–74.

Ra'Anan, Uri and C. M. Perry, eds. *Strategic Minerals and National Security.* Washington, DC: Pergamon-Brassey's, 1985.

Radetzki, Marian. "The Decline and Rise of the Multinational Corporation in the Metal Mineral Industry." *Resources Policy* 18, no. 1 (March 1992): 2–8.

―――. "Strategic Metal Markets: Prospects for Producer Cartels." *Resources Policy* 10, no. 4 (December 1984): 227–40.

―――. "Long Run Price Prospects for Aluminum and Copper." *Natural Resources Forum* 7 (1983): 23–36.

―――. *International Commodity Market Arrangements.* London: Hurst, 1970.

Radetzki, Marian and C. Van Duyne. "The Response of Mining Investment to a Decline in Economic Growth: The Case of Copper in the 1970s." *Journal of Development Economics* 15 (1984): 19–45.

Ramani, R. V., ed. *Application of Computer Methods in the Mineral Industry.* Proceedings of the 14th Symposium, October 4–8, 1976. New York: Society of Mining Engineers of American Institute of Mining, Metallurgical and Petroleum Engineers, Inc.

Ramsey, R. H. "The Snarl in Stockpiling Means Trouble for You." *Engineering and Mining Journal* (September 1949): 72–75.

Rausser, Gordon C., ed. *New Directions in Econometric Modeling and Forecasting in U.S. Agriculture.* New York: Elsevier, 1982.

Rausser, Gordon C., et al. "Developments in the Theory and Empirical Application of Endogenous Government Behavior." In *New Directions in Econometric Modeling and Forecasting in U.S. Agriculture*, edited by Gordon C. Rausser. New York: Elsevier, 1982.

Raw Materials Group. *Who Owns Who in Mining.* London: Roskill Information Services, 1992.

―――. *Structural Changes in the World Minerals Industry During the 1980s.* Study prepared for UNCTAD. Stockholm: Raw Materials Group, 1991.

Rees, Judith. *Natural Resources: Allocation, Economics and Policy.* London/New York: Routledge, 1990.

"Resource Firms Face Grim Reality: But Impact May Be Diminished as Canada Weans Itself off Commodities." *Financial Post* (July 10, 1993).

"Resource Wars: The Myth of American Vulnerability." *Business and Society Review* (Winter 1986): 38–45.

Rieber, Michael. "Level Playing Fields, Tilted Playing Fields and U.S. Competitiveness." *Resources Policy* 19, no. 4 (December 1993): 235–46.

Robbins, Peter. *Investing in Strategic Metals.* London: Strategic Metals Corporation, 1981.

Roberts, Peter W. and Tim Shaw. *Mineral Resources in Regional and Strategic Planning.* Westmead, Hampshire: Gower, 1982.

Robertson, William. *Tin: Its Production and Marketing.* London: Croom Helm, 1982.

―――. *Report on the World Tin Position with Projections for 1965 and 1970.* The Hague: International Tin Council, 1965.

Rodman, Kenneth A. *Sanctity vs. Sovereignty: The U.S. and the Nationalization of Natural Resource Investments.* New York: Columbia University Press, 1988.

Rodrik, D. "Managing Resource Dependency: The U.S. and Japan in the Markets for Copper, Iron Ore and Bauxite." *World Development* 10, no. 7 (July 1982): 541–60.

Rogich, Donald G. "Changing Minerals and Material Use Patterns." Speech presented to the Recycling Council of Ontario's 15th Annual Conference, October 5–7, 1994, Hamilton, Ontario (mimeo).

Rummel, R. J. "U.S. Foreign Relations: Conflict, Cooperation, and Attribute Distances." In *Peace, War, and Numbers*, edited by Bruce Russett. Beverly Hills, CA: Sage, 1972.

Russett, Bruce. "Dimensions of Resource Dependence: Some Elements of Rigor in Concept and Policy Analysis." *International Organization* 38 (Summer 1984): 481–99.

———. "Data Priorities for Modeling Global Dependence." In *Problems of World Modeling*, edited by K. Deutsch, et al. Cambridge: Ballinger, 1977.

———. "The Revolt of the Masses: Public Opinion on Military Expenditures." In *Peace, War and Numbers*, edited by Bruce Russett. Beverley Hills, CA: Sage, 1972.

———. *Peace, War, and Numbers.* Beverly Hills, CA: Sage, 1972.

Salamon, Lester M. and J. J. Siegfried. "Economic Power and Political Influence: The Impact of Industry Structure on Public Policy." *American Political Science Review* 71 (1977): 1026–43.

Salant, Stephen W. "The Vulnerability of Price Stabilization Schemes to Speculative Attacks." *Journal of Political Economy* 91, no. 1 (February 1983): 1–38.

———. "Staving Off the Backstop: Dynamic Limit Pricing with a Kinked Demand Curve." In *The Production and Pricing of Energy Resources*, edited by Robert S. Pindyck. Greenwich, CT: JAI Press, 1978.

Salant, Stephen W. and D. W. Henderson. "Market Anticipations of Government Policies and the Price of Gold." *Journal of Political Economy* 86, no. 4 (1978): 627–48.

Sanford, Jonathan. "Congressional Testimony by Foreign Officials and Citizens." *Library of Congress Study*, reprinted in *Congressional Record* 15 (June 1976): E3346–47.

Scherer, F.M. *Industrial Market Structure and Economic Performance.* Chicago: Rand McNally, 1980.

"Setback for Seaga: Reynolds Says Goodbye." *Multinational Monitor* 5, no. 4 (April 1984): 4.

Shafer, Michael. "Mineral Myths." *Foreign Policy* (Summer 1982): 154–71.

"The Shifting Stockpile Strategy: Carter's Plan, Adding to the Stockpile, Has Industry and Congress Balking." *Business Week* (September 26, 1977): 57.

Sibley, Scott F. "Cobalt: A Strategic and Critical Resource for Industrialized Nations, Supplied by Developing Nations." *Natural Resources Forum*, vol. 4 (1980): 403–13.

Singer, J. D. and M. Small. *Resort to Arms: International and Civil Wars, 1816–1980.* Beverley Hills, CA: Sage, 1982.

———. *The Wages of War.* New York: Wiley, 1972.

Slade, Margaret. "The Two Pricing Systems for Non–Ferrous Metals." *Resources Policy*, vol. 15 no. 3, September 1989, pp. 209–20.

———. *Pricing of Metals.* Kingston, Ontario: Queens University Centre for Resource Studies, 1988.

Smith, George David. *From Monopoly to Competition: The Transformations of Alcoa, 1888–1986.* New York: Cambridge University Press, 1988.

Smith, Gordon W. "Commodity Instability and Market Failure: A Survey of Issues." In *Stabilizing World Commodity Markets*, edited by F. G. Adams and S. Klein. Lexington, MA: Heath, 1978.

Smith, Gordon W. and G. R. Schink. "The International Tin Agreement: A Reassessment." *Economic Journal* (December 1976): 715–28.
"Stockpile Threat Lends Uncertainty to Cobalt Markets." *Northern Miner* 1 (December 1967): 1.
"Strategic Minerals: Private Stockpiles." *The Economist* 5 (December 1981).
"Strategic Minerals: Running the Risk." *The Economist* 12 (June 1980): 75.
"Strategic Stockpiles: Who's Hoarding What?" *The Economist* 24 (May 1980): 87–88.
Strongman, J. E., W. R. Killingsworth, and W. E. Cummings. "The Dynamics of the International Copper System." In *Application of Computer Methods in the Mineral Industry*, edited by R. V. Ramani. New York: American Institute of Mining, Metallurgical, and Petroleum Engineers, Inc., 1976.
"Struggling Producers." *South* (May 1983): 72.
Studies on Economic Stockpiling. Washington, DC: National Commission on Supplies and Shortages, September 1976.
Szuprowicz, Bohdan O. *How to Avoid Strategic Materials Shortages*. New York: Wiley, 1981.
Takeuchi, K. "CIPEC and the Copper Export Earnings of Member Countries." *The Developing Economies* 10, no. 1 (March 1972): 3–29.
Thoburn, John. *Multinationals, Mining, and Development: A Study of the Tin Industry*. Westmead, Hampshire: Gower, 1981.
Thoburn, John T. *Primary Commodity Exports and Economic Development*. New York: Wiley, 1977.
Thompson, William R. and Gary Zuk. "War, Inflation, and the Kondratieff Long Wave." *Journal of Conflict Resolution* 26 (1982): 621–44.
Tilton, John. "The Choice of Trading Partners: An Analysis of International Trade in Aluminum, Bauxite, Copper, Lead, Manganese, Tin and Zinc." *Yale Economic Essays* 6, no. 2 (Fall 1966): 419–74.
Tilton, John E. *Mineral Wealth and Economic Development*. Washington: Resources for the Future, 1992.
———. *World Mineral Exploration: Trends and Economic Issues*. Washington DC: Resources for the Future, 1988.
———. "Cyclical Instability: A Growing Threat to Metal Producers and Consumers." *Natural Resources Forum* 5 (1981): 5–14.
———. "Impact of Market Instability for Mineral Materials." *The World Economy* 1, no. 4 (October 1978): 369–83.
Tilton, John E., ed. *World Metal Demand: Trends and Prospects*. Washington, DC: Resources for the Future, 1991.
Tilton, J. E., R. G. Eggert and H. H. Landsberg. *World Mineral Exploration: Trends and Economic Issues*. Washington, DC: Resources for the Future, 1988.
"Tin: New Battle Lines Drawn." *South* (August 1982): 75–76.
"Tin Producers and Buyers Battle on the International Market—U.S. Accused of Foul Play." *Multinational Monitor* 3, no. 4 (April 1982): 8.
Tin Statistics 1966–1976. London: International Tin Council, 1977.
Tinsley, C. Richard. "Computer Applications of Non-Ferrous Econometric Models from the Raw Materials Consumer Perspective." In *Application of Computer Methods in the Mineral Industry*, edited by R. V. Ramani. New York: Society of Mining Engineers of the American Institute of Mining, Metallurgical, and Petroleum Engineers, Inc., 1977.

Turnovsky, Stephen J. "The Distribution of Welfare Gains from Price Stabilization: A Survey of Some Theoretical Issues." In *Stabilizing World Commodity Markets*, edited by F. G. Adams and S. Klein. Lexington, MA: Heath, 1978.

"U.K. Stockpiles Certain Metals." *Globe and Mail* (March 15, 1983), Toronto.

UNCTAD. Trade and Development Board. *Exploitation of the Mineral Resources of the Sea-Bed Beyond National Jurisdiction: Issues of International Commodity Policy.* New York: UNCTAD, 1973. (TD/B/449/Add.1)

U.N. Department for Economic and Social Information and Policy Analysis. Statistics Division. *International Trade Statistics Yearbook.* New York: United Nations, annual. (ST/ESA/STAT/SER.G/43)

U.N. Department of International Economic and Social Affairs. *Price Forecasting Techniques and Their Application to Minerals and Metals in the Global Economy.* New York: United Nations, 1984. (ST/ESA/140, E.84.II.C.3)

U.S. Bureau of Mines. *Minerals Yearbook.* Washington, DC: Bureau of Mines, annual.

U.S. Bureau of Mines. Office of Minerals Policy Analysis. *Chromium: Effectiveness of Alternative U.S. Policies in Reducing the Economic Costs of a Supply Disruption.* Washington, DC: Bureau of Mines, 1981.

"U.S. Commodity Policy and the Tin Agreement." In *The New International Economic Order: A U.S. Response*, edited by David B. H. Denoon. London: Macmillan, 1980.

U.S. Congress. *Assessment of Alternative Stockpiling Policies.* Report prepared for the House Science and Technology Committee, 94th Congress, 2nd session, August 1976. (J952-3)*

————. *Congressional Record*, April 3, 1979.

————. House of Representatives. Agriculture Committee. *International Sugar Stabilization Act of 1978.* Conference Report on H.R. 13750, 95th Congress, 2nd session, October 15, 1978. (H163-31)

————. House of Representatives. Armed Services Committee. *Full Committee Consideration of H. Res. 287 and General Services Administration Proposed Acquisition of Metallurgical Grade Bauxite (Jamaican Type).* 97th Congress, 1st session, December 9, 1981. (H201-7)

————. House of Representatives. Armed Services Committee. *Strategic and Critical Materials Transaction Authorization Act of 1979.* December 4, 1979. (H203-25)

————. House of Representatives. Armed Services Committee. *Disposal of Tin from the U.S. Strategic Stockpile.* March 20, 1979. (H203-2)

————. House of Representatives. Armed Services Committee. *Hearings: Full Committee Consideration of H.R. 9486 and Reprogramming Request No. FY 78-14.* 95th Congress, 2nd session, May 23, 1978. (H201-20)

————. House of Representatives. Armed Services Committee. *Amending the Strategic and Critical Materials Stock Piling Act.* March 22, 1977. (H203-3)

————. House of Representatives. Armed Services Committee. *Full Committee Consideration of H.R. 4895.* March 17, 1977. (H201-6)

————. House of Representatives. Armed Services Committee. *Full Committee Consideration of H.R. 15081 and H.R. 15378.* September 8, 1976. (H201-44)

————. House of Representatives. Armed Services Committee. Subcommittee on Seapower and Strategic and Critical Materials. *Hearings: National Defense Stockpile.* 97th Congress, 1st session, June 2 and 4, 1981. (H201-36)

* The code number given in parentheses following each Congressional hearing citation is the CIS (Congressional Index Service) reference number for that hearing.

————. House of Representatives. Armed Services Committee. Subcommittee on Seapower and Strategic and Critical Resources. *Hearings on H.R. 2603, H.R. 2784, H.R. 2912, and H.R. 3364*. June 2 and 4, 1981. (H201-36)

————. House of Representatives. Armed Services Committee. Subcommittee on Seapower and Strategic and Critical Materials. *Hearing on H.R. 1325 and H.R. 3385 and H.R. 3384*. 96th Congress, 1st session, July 25, 1979. (H201-24)

————. House of Representatives. Armed Services Committee. Subcommittee on Seapower and Strategic and Critical Resources. *Hearing on H.R. 595, a Bill to Authorize the Disposal of 35,000 Tons of Tin from the U.S. Strategic Stockpile*. 96th Congress, 1st session, March 2, 1979. (H201-13)

————. House of Representatives. Armed Services Committee. Subcommittee on Seapower and Strategic and Critical Materials. *Hearing on H.R. 2154, a Bill to Authorize the Acquisition of Materials for the U.S. Strategic Stockpile*. 96th Congress, 1st session, February 23 and 28, 1979. (H201-12)

————. House of Representatives. Armed Services Committee. Subcommittee on Seapower and Strategic and Critical Resources. *The United States Contribution to the International Tin Buffer Stock*. May 31, 1978. (H203–12)

————. House of Representatives. Armed Services Committee. Subcommittee on Seapower and Strategic and Critical Materials. *Hearings on H.R. 9486, a Bill to Authorize a Contribution by the U.S. to the Tin Buffer Stock Established under the Fifth International Tin Agreement*. 95th Congress, 2nd session, May 15, 1978. (H201-21)

————. House of Representatives. Armed Services Committee. Subcommittee on Seapower and Strategic and Critical Materials. *Hearings on H.R. 4895, a Bill to Amend the Strategic and Critical Materials Stock Piling Act*. 95th Congress, 1st session, March 14, 1977. (H201-4)

————. House of Representatives. Armed Services Committee. Subcommittee on Seapower and Strategic and Critical Materials. *Hearing on H.R. 15081, a Bill to Amend the Strategic and Critical Materials Stock Piling Act*. 94th Congress, 2nd session, August 26 and September 1, 1976. (H201-43)

————. House of Representatives. Banking, Finance and Urban Affairs Committee. Subcommittee on Economic Stabilization. *Hearings on H.R. 9486, a Bill to Authorize a Contribution by the United States to the Tin Buffer Stock Established under the 5th International Tin Agreement*. 95th Congress, 2nd session, May 11, 1978. (H241-44)

————. House of Representatives. Foreign Affairs Committee. *The United States Contribution to the International Tin Buffer Stock*. April 17, 1978. (H463-5)

————. House of Representatives. Foreign Affairs Committee. Subcommittee on International Economic Policy and Trade. *Hearings: U.S. International Commodity Policy—Tin*. 95th Congress 2nd session, February 15, 16, 21 March 1, and April 5, 1978. (H461-41)

————. House of Representatives. Committee on Interior and Insular Affairs. Subcommittee on Mines and Mining. *U.S. Minerals Vulnerability: National Policy Implications*. 96th Congress, 2nd session, November 1980.

————. Joint Committee on Banking. *Hearings: Defense Industrial Base. Part 3: New Stockpile Objectives*. 94th Congress, 2nd session, November 24, 1976. (J821-5)

————. Joint Committee on Defense Production. *Hearings: Defense Industrial Base—New Stockpile Objectives*. November 24, 1976. (J821-5)

————. Joint Committee on Defense Production. Subcommittee on Materials Availability. *Hearings: The Purpose and Organization of Economic Stockpiling*. June 8 and 9, 1976. (J821-1)

————. Joint Committee—Office of Technology Assessment *Report. Assessment of Alternative Economic Stockpiling* Policies. August, 1976. (J952-23)

————. *Message from the President of the United States—Disposal of various Materials from the National Stockpile*. April 16, 1973.

————. Senate. Armed Services Committee. *Strategic and Critical Materials Transaction Authorization Act of 1979*. October 3, 1979. (S203-14)

————. Senate. Armed Services Committee. *National Defense Stockpile Act*. May 15, 1978. (S203-3)

————. Senate. Armed Services Committee. Subcommittee on Military Construction and Stockpiles. *Hearing: Stockpile Commodity Legislation*. 96th Congress, 1st session, July 10, 1979. (S201-25)

————. Senate. Armed Services Committee. Subcommittee on Military Construction and Stockpiles. *Hearing: Strategic and Critical Materials Stock Piling Act Revision*. 96th Congress, 1st session, March 19, 1979. (S201-7)

————. Senate. Armed Services Committee. Subcommittee on Military Construction and Stockpiles. *Hearings: Consideration of Stockpile Legislation*. 95th Congress, 2nd session, March 8 and 9, 1978. (S201-22)

————. Senate. Armed Services Committee. Subcommittee on Military Construction and Stockpiles. *Hearings: General Stockpile Policy*. 95th Congress, 1st session, September 9, 1977. (S201-1)

————. Senate. Committee on Armed Services. Subcommittee on National Stockpile and Naval Petroleum Reserves. *Hearing: Disposals from National and Supplemental Stockpiles*. 92nd Congress, 1st session, April 7, 1971. (9272)

————. Senate. Committee on Armed Services. Subcommittee on National Stockpile and Naval Petroleum Reserves. *Hearing: Disposals from National and Supplemental Stockpiles*. 91st Congress, 2nd session, February 27, 1970. (6787)

————. Senate. Committee on Banking, Housing and Urban Affairs. *Hearing on Strategic Stockpile Policy*. November 14, 1978. (S241-10)

————. Senate. Committee on Governmental Affairs. Subcommittee on Federal Spending Practices and Open Government. *GSA Contract Fraud Investigation*. June 23, 1978. (S401-32.3)

————. Senate. Committee on Interior and Insular Affairs. *Establishing a National Minerals Policy*. Reports No. 967 and 968, 1959. (16157, 16158)

————. Senate. Committee on Interior and Insular Affairs. Subcommittee on Minerals, Materials, and Fuels. *Hearings: Extension of Purchase Programs of Strategic and Critical Minerals*. 84th Congress, 2nd session, April 19, 20, 21, 25, May 16, 24, and 25, 1956. (12428)

————. Senate. Select Committee on Small Business. Subcommittee No. 2. *Hearings: Problems Resulting from the Exclusion of Small Business from Stockpile Purchases and from Participation in the Disposal of Surplus Products Program*. 84th Congress, 2nd session, July 11, 12, and 17, 1956. (18647)

————. Senate. *Strategic and Critical Materials Transaction Act of 1978*. June 7, 1978. (S203-5)

U.S. Department of Defense. *Report to the Congress on National Defense Stockpile Requirements*. Washington, DC: Department of Defense, various years.

————. *Strategic and Critical Materials Report to the Congress*. Washington, DC: Department of Defense, various years.

U.S. Department of the Interior. Office of Minerals Policy and Research Analysis. *Cobalt: Effectiveness of Alternative U.S. Policies of Reduce the Cost of a Supply Disruption.* Washington, DC: Department of the Interior, August 1981.

U.S. General Services Administration. Office of Finance. *Status of Defense Materials Inventories.* Washington, DC: General Services Administration, various years.

U.S. General Services Administration. Office of Preparedness. *Stockpile Report to the Congress.* Washington, DC: General Services Administration, various years.

"U.S. Planning to Buy Cobalt, Sell Its Silver." *Globe and Mail* (April 9, 1981): B15, Toronto.

"U.S. Tin Stockpile Talks Set for Next Week." *Financial Times* (July 29, 1982): 28.

Varon, Bension and Wolfgang Glushke. "Mineral Commodity Projections as a Tool for Planning." In *Application of Computer Methods in the Mineral Industry*, edited by R. V. Ramani. New York: Society of Mining Engineers of the American Institute of Mining, Metallurgical, and Petroleum Engineers, Inc., 1977.

Varon, Bension, Wolfgang Glushke, and Joseph Shaw. *Copper: The Next Fifteen Years.* United Nations Centre for Natural Resources, Energy, and Transport. Dordrecht, Holland: D. Reidel, 1979.

Vial, Joaquin. "Copper Consumption in the USA: Main Determinants and Structural Changes." *Resources Policy*, vol. 18 no. 2, June 1992, pp. 107–21.

Vogely, W. A., ed. *Mineral Materials Modeling.* Baltimore: Johns Hopkins, 1975.

Wade, N. "Raw Materials: U.S. Grows More Vulnerable to Third World Cartels." *Science* 183, no. 4121 (January 18, 1974): 185–86.

Wagenhals,Gerhard. "Econometric Models of Minerals Markets: Uses and Limitations." *Natural Resources Forum* 8, no. 1 (1984): 77–86.

———. *The World Copper Market: Structure and Econometric Model.* Berlin and New York: Springer Verlag, 1984.

Wallace, Michael D. "Old Nails in New Coffins: The Para Bellum Hypothesis Revisited." *Journal of Peace Research* 18, no. 1 (1981): 91–95.

———. "Arms Races and Escalation: Some New Evidence." *Journal of Conflict Resolution* 23, no. 1 (March 1979): 3–16.

———. *War and Rank Among Nations.* Lexington, MA: Lexington Books, 1973.

Wallace, Michael D. and J. M. Wilson. "Nonlinear Arms Race Models: A Test of Some Alternatives." *Journal of Peace Research* 15, no. 2 (1978): 175–92.

Weingast, Barry R. and Mark J. Moran. "Bureaucratic Discretion or Congressional Control? Regulatory Policymaking by the Federal Trade Commission." *Journal of Political Economy* 91, no. 5 (1983): 765–800.

"Why Jamaica's Economy May Run Around." *Business Week* 18 (October 1982): 162–63.

Wildavsky, Aaron. *The Politics of the Budgetary Process.* Boston: Little, Brown, 1964.

Wilkenfeld, Jonathan. "Models for the Analysis of Foreign Conflict Behaviour of States." In *Peace, War, and Numbers*, edited by Bruce Russett. Beverley Hills, CA: Sage, 1972.

Winters, L. Alan and David Sapsford. *Primary Commodity Prices: Economic Models and Policy.* Cambridge: Cambridge University Press, 1990.

Wolf, Jr., Charles. "Some Aspects of the 'Value' of Less-Developed Countries to the U.S." *World Politics* 15, no. 4 (July 1963): 623–34.

Woods, Douglas W. and James C. Burrows. *The World Aluminum-Bauxite Market.* New York: Praeger, 1980.

World Bank Commodity Models. World Bank Staff Commodity Working Paper 1, no. 6 (1981).

World Bank, Commodities and Export Projections Division, Economic Analysis and Pro-
jections Department, Economics and Research Staff. *Price Prospects for Major Pri-
mary Commodities*. Report No. 814/82. Volume I: Summary and Implications. Volume
IV: Metals and Minerals. Washington, DC: World Bank, 1982.
Zorn, Stephen A. "Producers Associations and Commodity Markets: The Case of CIPEC."
In *Stabilizing World Commodity Markets*, edited by F. G. Adams and S. Klein.
Lexington, MA: Lexington Books, 1978.

Index

About the Author

PATRICIA E. PERKINS is an Assistant Professor teaching environmental and ecological economics in the Faculty of Environmental Studies at York University in Ontario, Canada. Dr. Perkins has worked in Brazil and Mozambique, taught economics at several North American institutions, and has served as policy advisor for the Ontario Ministry of Environment and Energy.

ISBN 0-275-94258-9

90000>

EAN

9 780275 942588

HARDCOVER BAR CODE